Badger Boneyards

Enjoy this grave undertaking

Dennis McCann

Lake Superior
Minnesota
Superior
Bayfield
La Pointe,
Madeline Island
Washburn
Hurley
Presque Isle
Michigan
Norway, MI
Rhinelander
Medford
Menomonie
Eau Claire
Peshtigo
Fish
Creek
Green Bay
Namur
Brussels
WISCONSIN
Oneida
Stockbridge
Montello
Wisconsin Dells
Richland
Center
Sauk City
Spring
Green
Prairie
du Chien
McGregor,
IA
Mount
Horeb
Madison
Ixonia
Milwaukee
North
Andover
Rewey
Little
Prairie
Hazel Green
Iowa
Illinois
Lake Michigan

Mapping Specialists, Ltd.

Badger Boneyards

The Eternal Rest of the Story

Dennis McCann

Wisconsin Historical Society Press

Published by the Wisconsin Historical Society Press
Publishers since 1855

Publication of this book was made possible in part by a grant from the Amy Louise Hunter fellowship fund.

wisconsinhistory.org

Photographs by Barbara McCann, Dennis McCann, and Mark Fay

Printed in Wisconsin, U.S.A.

Designed by Will Capellaro

14 13 12 11 10   1 2 3 4 5

Library of Congress Cataloging-in-Publication Data

McCann, Dennis, 1950–
Badger boneyards : the eternal rest of the story / Dennis McCann.
p. cm.
ISBN 978-0-87020-451-7 (paper : alk. paper) 1. Cemeteries—Wisconsin. 2. Sepulchral monuments—Wisconsin. 3. Wisconsin—History, Local. 4. Wisconsin—History—Anecdotes. 5. Wisconsin—Biography—Anecdotes. I. Title.
F582.M395 2010
929'.5—dc22

2009047246

∞ The paper used in this publication meets the minimum requirements of the American National Standard for Information Sciences—Permanence of Paper for Printed Library Materials, ANSI Z39.48-1992.

For all of the dead
who give these stories life

Contents

Photo by Mark Fay

Preface

Some years ago while in Atlanta on important newspaper business—yes, there is still such a thing—I noticed in a visitor guide that the greatest amateur golfer ever, one Robert Tyre Jones, or Bobby to his friends, was buried in historic Oakland Cemetery.

This interested me for two reasons. One, I play golf. Jones, in addition to his spectacular playing career, founded the Masters Tournament, which is played each year at Augusta National Golf Club in Georgia. He was an iconic figure in the game. Two, on another occasion some friends and I had once spent an afternoon trying, quite unsuccessfully, to find the Atlanta house where Jones had lived.

I told Dale, the photographer I was with at the time, that we had to add Oakland Cemetery to our itinerary. Dale was not a golfer. He looked at me as if the fever had claimed my mind. It took two days to persuade him I was serious, but on our last day he agreed we could swing through the cemetery on our way to the airport. When we did, we found Jones's grave, mowed short and tight as a putting green and graced with eighteen specimens of plants, one for each hole at Augusta National Golf Course.

While Dale was less than reverent ("Instead of a hole in one," he said, "he's the one in a hole."), I briefly paid respects.

On top of housing the grave of Robert Jones, Oakland was a spectacular cemetery, a quiet city of some seventy thousand residents, with sections for Union soldiers and Confederate soldiers, a potter's field with seventeen thousand graves, a section for former slaves, a Jewish section, and even a marker for Tweet the Mockingbird. There was so much grand Victorian funerary architecture as to put Oakland Cemetery on the National Register of Historic Places.

On our way out I saw a sign pointing to the grave of Margaret Mitchell, of *Gone with the Wind* fame, and asked Dale if we shouldn't stop there as well.

"Frankly," he said, "I don't give a damn."

I forgave him that, but I surely didn't agree.

Cemeteries have long held interest for me, which may be odd given my intention to one day be cremated and—nice coincidence here—gone with the wind myself. Maybe this interest stems from my college years, when I sometimes mowed grass in a small cemetery in a town settled by Norwegian immigrants. Amid row after row of stones with Norwegian names was a marker for one lonely Irishman named Louis Kelly, an oddity I wove into a newspaper column years later, when I discovered Shamrock, Wisconsin.

As a traveling newspaperman I often found stories in cemeteries the way political reporters find them at city hall or sports reporters find them in a gym. In Taos, New Mexico, I stood at the grave of Kit Carson, whose frontier exploits had intrigued me as a child. In Key West, I went early one morning to the historic cemetery where the dead are buried both above and below ground to see the monument to the U.S.S. *Maine* and the famous headstone of B. P. "Pearl" Roberts, who was said to have been a hypochondriac. Her husband ordered a marker that read, "I told you I was sick."

In Savannah, Georgia, visiting Bonaventure Cemetery was as much a must-do as trying the southern specialty called she-crab soup, and it's hard to say which I savored more. Bonaventure is the gorgeous, atmospheric burial place made widely famous in John Berendt's *Midnight in the Garden of Good and Evil*, but it had been discovered long before that. John Muir, after five days camping there in 1867, declared it "so beautiful that almost any sensible person would choose to dwell here with the dead rather than with the lazy, disorderly living."

Preface

It might sound funny to say the dead have inspired a lot of stories for me, but it's true.

In Benton, Wisconsin, in the lead mine region, I once stopped at the grave of the celebrated pioneer priest Father Samuel Mazzuchelli, whose Italian name was said to have so challenged the Irish nuns with whom he worked that they called him Father Mathew Kelly instead. Sure enough, his grave is flanked by those of several nuns with Irish names, all residents of St. Patrick's Catholic Cemetery.

In the cemetery in the little town of Scandinavia, I once tried to count the number of Nelsons under grass, but I gave up when I couldn't find a story in that. In New Diggings (the name refers to digging for lead, not graves) I walked through the old Masonic Cemetery, said to be the first Masonic burial yard in Wisconsin and a reminder that rites mattered, even in the state's rugged early days.

In Michigan's Upper Peninsula I spent an afternoon poking through Irish Hollow Cemetery, where it occurred to me that the cemetery that survives a ghost town must be doubly haunted. And one of my favorite interviews ever, retold in this collection, came years ago in a cemetery on the Wisconsin-Michigan border, where an old-time sexton nicknamed Digger gave me the lowdown as only an old-time sexton nicknamed Digger could:

"You got to be a cemetery man," he said. "You got to be dedicated. You got to go with the weather. When there's snow, you know, or a goddarn rainstorm you got to be out there, you got to get that goddarn thing in the ground. If the man says the funeral is ten o'clock Tuesday it's ten o'clock Tuesday.

"Even though you are dead, you are on time."

There are thousands of cemeteries in Wisconsin, large and small, tidy and neglected, so old the headstones can't tell their stories and so new the ground is still wet from the tears of mourners. For every sprawling city of the dead such as Milwaukee's Forest Home Cemetery, with more than one hundred thousand burials, there is a bedroom-size family plot on a country road. In either case, and in every cemetery in between, wherever the dead rest, history lives.

An Old-Time Cemetery Man

Norway, Michigan

This story comes from about six feet over the Wisconsin-Michigan border, but no artificial boundary should get in the way of a good cemetery tale. Someone once told me when I got to this area I should slip across the border and visit Digger.

Digger is really Ed Wenzel, but also called Billy. He was seventy-six when we met in the early 1990s and might truly be called the last of a dying breed: a small-town sexton who knows where the bodies are buried, because he buried them.

When I called to say I was coming I was struck by Digger's distinctive U.P. accent, so I bought a tape recorder that night and took it with me the next day. Digger was wearing a cap and work clothes, but with no immediate need to arrange for another permanent lodger he had time to show me around the piney setting where he worked.

I'd been told to ask Digger about the old days, so I did.

> 1937. April the first, 1937.
>
> When I walked up here the first day, it was really like a son of a gun. You had to walk four miles, there was no cars them days. There was no building, nothing. Just a little old shed down in a hole. They had a wheelbarrow, a shovel, and a rake, that's all they had. Steel wheel, too.

You had to dig everything by hand, and then wheel everything to the woods by wheelbarrow, because there's half the grave left over. Anybody with common sense knows that. . . .

Like I said, you had no place to eat, no shed, thirty below you had to come out and dig. You had to shovel the snow by hand, no snow-blow, all with a scoop shovel. Then I started to plow with a truck without no door. That's how I froze my face. . . .

[I got] a dollar and a half a day, and then the other guys got a dollar and a quarter. I got a quarter more because I took the foreman's job. I did it all, take care of the books, the whole damn thing. And I never was a bookkeeper, I was a grave digger and I told 'em that. Now I get, well, a guy shouldn't put salaries in there. . . .

We only get $325 here for digging a grave. They get six and eight hundred in Iron Mountain. . . . See, we don't have no backhoe. We could have one, but to me it don't seem feasible. It's only sand, you know.

We dig 'em all by hand. Couple of hours in the sand and we dig a hole, and one hour after we're done . . . you couldn't even tell where he was buried. We dig 'em all year round. I dug at thirty below. You gotta pound with a hammer and maul and dig 'em. When you're young you can go like heck. Like I said, it's sand . . . but like I said, it ain't easy.

And I hate to say it but if I hadn't never stayed here they wouldn't have the cemetery like it is. I don't want to brag about myself, but I know, because I keep this up like I keep my yard at home.

But I'm only one man and I'm getting older. I can't cut the mustard like I used to. Because I fell off the roof five years ago and about killed myself.

My wife rolled me over and I heard her long miles away saying, "Eddy, your father's gone, I think. I think your father is gone, go call the ambulance. I think your poor, old father is dead." But then I started to roll a bit. She said, "Oh Lord amighty, he's starting to move."

A woman the other day said, "I never thought you'd be back digging holes again, you were pretty well battered." I broke my arm and my collarbone and my pelvis, but I got out of the damn bed and came back and dug again.

An Old-Time Cemetery Man

> You got to be a cemetery man. You got to be dedicated. You got to go with the weather. When there's snow, you know, or a goddarn rainstorm you got to be out there, you got to get that goddarn thing in the ground. If the man says the funeral is ten o'clock Tuesday it's ten o'clock Tuesday. Even though you are dead, you are on time.

We sat for a while in the sexton's office, where large historic photographs served as decor.

> Oh yeah, all the miners from that top picture up there, I buried the whole damn bunch of them. Even the widows, now, because that's fifty-five years now, don't forget. See, all these younger guys—this kid'll be in here in a little while, funny he ain't here already—they're dead, all these guys. . . .
>
> My mother, my father, my brothers, I did. I dug my mother's on Sunday. I dug all my relations, too. It never bothered me. Yesterday I buried my classmate. When [someone] calls up and says so-and-so's dead, you kind of feel funny. You get used to it, like anything else.
>
> Years ago, I done all the digging but now I get [my son Eddy] and them kids, they like that, see. . . .
>
> But I know when I'm gone, the day I walk out of here, they're going to go mechanized, I know they are.

We drove to the cemetery, where I met a host of dead people. "The first grave I dug was right there," Billy would say, a man at peace with his accomplishments.

He is at home here, and like a good cemetery man he has planned ahead. His stone is in place, and he knows who will open the earth to receive him.

"Eddy," he said. Like father, like son.

Photo by Mark Fay

An old gravestone in Fish Creek, Wis.

Buried in a Peninsular Paradise
Fish Creek

Visitors come by the thousands to Door County's popular Peninsula State Park, in summer to camp and hike and bike or play golf, and when winter thins the blood they come to ski and snowshoe.

And, in all seasons, some come to visit the dead. It may surprise those who think of a state park as a place of pleasure to learn there are two cemeteries within the boundaries of Peninsula Park, as well as an Indian leader buried beneath a totem pole on the state-owned golf course and yet another cemetery on private property adjacent to the park's northern entrance in Ephraim. A pause to take them in will reveal a lot about the peninsula's early days.

The oldest graveyard is the pioneer family cemetery tucked among the brush and trees at Weborg Point, not far from the park's Fish Creek gateway. It would be easy to miss it entirely, so obscured is it by growth, but look hard for the metal arch and small fieldstone fence—the classic boundary in Door County—and there you will find the graves of some of the area's earliest white settlers, the Claflins and the Thorps.

According to John M. Kahlert's most informative *Pioneer Cemeteries: Door County Wisconsin*, a book any cemetery buff should seek out, the oldest marked grave in the cemetery (that of Sarah Ann Claflin, who died in 1850) is also among the oldest in Door County. Another marker refers to the "children of Increase and Mary Ann Claflin," though most of the other markers are for the Thorps, who arrived in Door County about ten years after Increase Claflin moved to Fish Creek in 1844.

Increase Claflin died in 1858 and supposedly was buried in the cemetery, Kahlert wrote, though in an unmarked grave. Two of his three sons, Albert and Charles, are buried under a double marker that notes their military service in the Civil War.

Blossomburg Cemetery, in the middle of Peninsula Park, is much larger and more noticeable; while it is not as old as the pioneer cemetery, it is well worth inspecting, as a number of bicyclists were on the summer day I last visited. It is, as can be said of many cemeteries, a most pleasant site, bordered on three sides by woods and graced with its own tall trees for shade. If one must be buried, there are worse places than a grassy opening in the middle of this piney peninsular park.

According to Kahlert, the cemetery was established to serve the residents of the town of Gibraltar and got its unusual name when an old Scandinavian named Ole Klugeland, who was familiar with the strong gales that blew across pretty Eagle Harbor, called it "Blaasenberg," or Windy Mountain. "It was not long before, in common parlance, it became Blossomburg," Kahlert said.

Blossomburg's oldest graves date to the late 1800s, and some prominent Door County names are present and accounted for. Hjalmer Holand, whose *Old Peninsula Days* history of the county is still a popular seller with tourists, is there, as is the former sheriff, Hollis J. Brindenhagen, whose stone is rough-cut in the distinctive shape of Door County and boasts a six-pointed sheriff's star and his dates of service, 1962–1982. Yet another marker includes an etching of the popular supper club Sister Bay Bowl.

I was brought up short by one grave, which had only recently been dug and occupied. Leaning against the stone were two plastic leg braces, women's worn brown shoes still attached and obviously no longer needed. I liked the statement they made, even if I couldn't be entirely certain what it was.

As always, some markers are cryptic, sharing no more than names and dates. But Vito Demarinis, who died in 2001 at age seventy-five, received his due:

We'll remember
His smile
His laughter
His love.
The good times
And the bad,
His garden
The vegetables
The gladiolas
His pizza!
His love!

Not many markers get exclamation points. It must have been wonderful pizza.

I don't often walk onto a golf course without clubs over my shoulder, but I made an exception in order to visit the resting place of Simon Kahquados, the respected Potawatomi leader buried under the Indian Memorial Pole between the first and ninth holes at Peninsula State Park Golf Course.

The marker on a large rock near the pole reads, "A true and worthy Indian."

For tourist-dependent Door County, he was also a true and worthy opportunity, and how he ended up buried on a golf course is a pretty good yarn.

The memorial pole arrived before Simon Kahquados did. It was erected in 1927 as a tribute to the Potawatomi Indians who had lived in Door County before white settlement. Kahlert said it was the writer and local history buff Hjalmer Holand's idea to have the pole carved with Potawatomi designs—never mind that such totem poles were not part of Potawatomi tradition but more associated with tribes in the northwestern United States and British Columbia. Door County being Door County, the pole's dedication was widely publicized, and a nice crowd of tourists attended, as did a party of Potawatomi from their reservation in Forest County.

One was Simon Onanguisse Kahquados, who was usually described as the last descendant of a long line of Potawatomi chiefs who had presided in Door County. He was born in 1851 in Mishicot, where his parents were visiting, but his father was from the Mink River area of Door County. Kahquados grew up hunting and fishing, later learned to read and write, and worked for many years in the timber business in Michigan as a timber cruiser, estimating forest yields. He married and had nine children and eventually returned to Wisconsin, where he became involved in tribal matters and was a leader of his people, arguing for fair treatment of Indians by federal agencies.

He never lost his love for Door County. He was seventy-six when he presided over the pole's dedication with what Kahlert called "a moving speech," and when he was offered a chance to one day be buried at the pole's base he eagerly accepted. On November 27, 1930, Simon Kahquados died, a victim of the same poverty he had sought to erase among his people. The *Sheboygan Press* noted the sadness of "succumbing to disease in his poor hovel after months of suffering and want.

"That this old chief of the Potawatomis, in poor health, at an advanced age, and unable to work, had to subsist on a pittance of $10 a month is a reproach to the federal government for its failure to give its wards adequate care."

Door County would keep its promise to Kahquados, if not immediately. Because he died in the middle of winter, arrangements were made to keep the body in a morgue in Wabeno so his burial could take place at a time more convenient for tourists to attend

Photo by Mark Fay

Potawatomi leader Simon Kahquados is buried beneath this totem pole at Peninsula State Golf Course.

and, not coincidentally, spend a few dollars. But better weather was also an argument. As the *Sheboygan Press* said in urging readers to attend, "This is a fine time of the year to make such a trip[,] considering that it is 'Cherry Blossom Time' in Door County, and the trees are in full bloom."

The Door County Historical Society, State Conservation Commission, State Historical Society, and other agencies were all represented at the 1931 Memorial Day weekend ceremony, as were Potawatomi leaders who served as pallbearers. Simon was buried in a coat he had worn to Washington and to Madison to lobby for his people; a gun, powder, peace pipe, beads, tribal headgear, and other traditional possessions accompanied him as well.

According to a later account, a tribal elder visiting the grave in the 1960s was upset that Kahquados had been buried on a golf course, but, to take the longer view, at least he was buried in the heart of the place he loved best.

The original pole was replaced in 1970 and again in 1994. Given the tall trees on the site, it would be easy to play the course without noticing the pole or Simon Kahquados's resting place. But those who play the course should at least tip a cap his way. Where else will a golfer who hits a wayward shot find a local rule that invites them to "take relief from the totem pole area on #9"?

Where Oles Go to Rest
Mount Horeb

Some years ago I gave a talk to a group in Milwaukee. As I often did, I read from a favorite old column about a cemetery near Stoughton where a solitary Irishman, Louis Kelly, was inexplicably buried among some one hundred and fifty Norwegians (including seven named Ole) and how I later found another cemetery in tiny Shamrock, in western Wisconsin, where poor lonely Louis the Irishman probably should have been laid to rest.

Afterward, a member of the audience told me about a monument to Norwegian settlers in a field near a historic church outside of Mount Horeb, in western Dane County, and said I should make a visit. I said I would, so he later sent me directions.

It took me five years to get there, which I attribute more to the press of business than indolence and lethargy.

But that's the thing about the dead: they wait for you.

When I did come across those directions in a file of old mail and went off to keep my promise, everything was just as described.

As it turned out, I knew the church in question. Springdale Lutheran Church, just outside of Mount Horeb and about twenty miles from Madison, is one of the well-known sights in that rolling countryside, a classic white country church with a twenty-five-foot steeple. It stands on the site where pioneer Norwegians built their first house of worship in 1861, a few years after they began to arrive in large numbers to build farms in Dane County.

"Following the Norwegian tradition," a historical marker in front declares, "they built their church on a hill." In 1895 the current structure replaced the original church, but the steeple from the first building was placed on top of the new to preserve a link to the congregation's roots. Aslak Olson Lie, a skilled cabinetmaker, painter, and metal worker who led a group of Norwegians there in 1848, was thought to have been involved in the design of the steeple, modeling it and other features after his home church in Norway.

Even without the sign in front, a first-time visitor would know the congregation's roots were Norwegian. Carved in stone in the cemetery next to the church are such names as Thore Thoreson, Thor Thorson, Tosten Thompson, Halvor Bangs, Peter Peterson, and Andrew Anderson.

And, of course, there are almost enough Oles to field an all-Ole baseball team—Ole Lee and Ole Johnson, Ole Brager and Ole Bortness, Oles Dahl, Gorden, Grinde, and Rockstad. All have grand views of the Dane County countryside, and I would have stayed to enjoy it with them but for a lacerating January wind and an icy road that prevented all but tiptoe passage.

More important, it wasn't the cemetery I had come to see.

According to my directions, the Norwegian monument was nearly a mile away, and it took a while to find it. From the church I drove three-tenths of a mile north on Town Hall Road, where an old newsletter from the Springdale Association had said if I carefully scanned the ridges to the northwest I might see it "standing like a steeple amongst the corn. . . ."

I looked, and looked hard, but even without corn I couldn't see it. So I drove farther to the north, turned onto a dead end marked "Norwegian Trail," and looked again, still without luck. It wasn't until I knocked on a farmhouse door and inquired of the woman who answered that my fortune changed. She pointed over my shoulder and across the road, and there it was on the top of a rise.

Standing like a steeple.

It marks a cemetery that was, but isn't really anymore. From 1847, the year before statehood, to 1863, after the new church and cemetery had been established, more than fifty members of the pioneer community were buried on that rise. They were remembered with wooden crosses, but time and the elements gradually erased those. In 1901 the seventeen-foot granite-and-limestone obelisk was placed on the site, and those known to be buried there are named on the marker's base: Soren Sorenson, in the Norwegian way, and four more Oles among them.

Driving back to the church, I stopped again at the point where I had tried with no success to see the marker. This time I could make it out, even against the backdrop of trees that had hidden it earlier. When summer comes the tall corn might make it invisible, I suppose, but corn comes and goes.

Not like the marker, and the memories it keeps.

Photo by Mark Fay

Daniel Ninham is said to be the first Oneida born in Wisconsin.

Listen to Me, Just Once
Oneida

Many Wisconsin cemeteries boast the graves of Civil War soldiers, including a few with Confederates at rest. But veterans of the Revolutionary War are rather rare in a state that would not exist until decades after American freedom was won. Rarer still is the grave of an Indian who fought on the American side.

There is one, though, at the lovely hillside cemetery next to historic Holy Apostles Episcopal Church in Brown County, and on Freedom Road to boot. And as one might guess, James Powlis took a circuitous path to his eternal resting place.

He is remembered not by a grave marker but by an official state historical marker that tells more than mere name and dates. Powlis was an Oneida Indian who was born around 1750 in New York State (his Oneida name was said to have translated to "I'm Worried," which seems odd, but an official historical marker can't make stuff up, right?). An Oneida chief, he joined the Continental Army in 1777 after Congress offered army commissions and American protection and supplies in an effort to win over the Oneidas.

In 1779 Congress resolved that twelve Oneida and Tuscarora chiefs be commissioned as Officers of the Line in the Continental Army; Powlis was made a captain and served with Lieutenant

Colonel Louis Cook, a Mohawk who was the highest-ranking Indian in the army. Powlis was honorably discharged in 1784 and received a grant of eighteen hundred acres in New York State as his pension for military service. He moved to Wisconsin after his wife's death and died at Oneida in 1849 at age ninety-nine. His headstone is gone, but a historical marker states that Powlis is believed to have been buried in the family plot, along with relatives who may have been part of the large migration of Oneidas from New York.

Holy Apostles Cemetery, one of the oldest in the region, holds other interesting burials as well. Holy Apostles Church, in fact, was founded in New York in 1702 and brought to Wisconsin in 1822. Reverend Eleazer Williams, the so-called Lost Dauphin who led a group of Oneida Indians from New York to build new homes in then largely unsettled Wisconsin, later died in New York. However, his remains and—according to the book *Historic Northeast Wisconsin*—his headstone were brought back to Wisconsin to be reinterred in the churchyard of Holy Apostles. His marker is set a bit apart from the rest of the cemetery, close to the church, as is the marker for Cornelius Hill, 1834–1907, "Last chief and first priest of the Oneidas."

The cemetery runs along a sometimes-steep hillside that offers grand views of the countryside outside of Green Bay. A cemetery worker, Mike Smith, who described himself as a full-blooded Oneida, said the views are so beautiful that some visitors come with books to sit and read and take in the scenery. The spot is sufficiently popular that there are plans to put out benches for visitors' comfort.

Sitting is nice, but walking among the stones is more interesting and instructive. So many graves bear military markers that the "warrior tradition" of the Oneida people is immediately evident. In the back of the cemetery, near the tree line, is a stone for Daniel Ninham, said to be the first Oneida born in Wisconsin, in 1827. And the marker for Thomas King remembers "a chief of the First Christian Party of the Oneida Nation."

There are more personal touches on these graves than in most cemeteries. Many graves include the nicknames of those

Photo by Barbara McCann

The grave of Roy Kenneth Metoxen in Oneida, Wis.

underground; the marker of "Cookie" Jourdan, whose given name was Emerson, shows etchings of Sylvester and Tweety Bird. Others bear dream catchers, etchings of deer or bears reflecting native pride, musical notes, linked wedding rings, and writing in the Oneida language. Of course there are graves bearing the Green Bay Packers *G*—even one with a glass photo of the deceased wearing a Packers stocking cap.

The wooden marker for Roy Kenneth Metoxen shows both carved bears and a veteran's star and reads, "Listen to me, just once." It was impossible to say whom that was meant for, whether wife, children, coworkers, or even the government, but it seemed to reveal a man who felt his wisdom to be underappreciated. At least in death he got the last word, so while I doubted he had intended the epitaph for me, I stood on the hillside and listened anyway.

Sorry, Roy. I heard nothing but the song of birds and the summer breeze drifting through the air. But it was nice—as lovely as the pastoral panorama provided for the dead to enjoy, if only they could.

The Boneyard Built by Barons
Menomonie

There are, as you would expect, some ostentatious markers in this cemetery that dates to the region's lumber-era glory days, but it was a relatively modest and circumspect stone that drew my eye.

Carolyn Ohnstad, Evergreen Cemetery's superintendent, biggest booster, and rules enforcer, paused by the stone as we neared the end of our tour.

"Bye," the marker reads. "Rest in Peace."

I thought it mighty neighborly of a cemetery to offer such parting salutations, though I offered that "Bye—Drive Safely" might have worked as well. But no, Ohnstad said, the deceased's actual name was Bye.

Perfect, because as farewells go, "Bye—Rest in Peace" works just fine.

Evergreen has been a place for final farewells for more than one hundred and thirty years, dating to the boom times of the great northern forest. The harvest of white pine, hemlock, and other species was like a gold rush for this part of Dunn County, and the largest player in the game was the famed Knapp, Stout & Company, organized in 1853. In addition to running lumber mills at full production, Knapp, Stout owned stores, farms, gardens, and shopping spaces.

While those concerns provided services to the still-upright

population of Menomonie and surrounding towns, any industry as dangerous as lumbering and mill work would soon create a need for public conveniences for the eternally inconvenienced. In 1873, Knapp, Stout began a movement to create a cemetery association and newspaper ads urged citizens to attend meetings to make such plans.

Perhaps not surprisingly in a town where one company ran so many endeavors, citizens left the task of cemetery creation to Knapp, Stout. Give them this: the company did not take the easy way out and plow up a stumpy cutover patch of land to serve as resting place for the city.

Quite the opposite. Knapp, Stout produced a cemetery that would eventually merit inclusion on the Wisconsin and National Registers of Historic Places. They set aside about thirty-five acres overlooking the mill pond and hired Cleveland and French, landscape architects from Chicago, to plat a cemetery in keeping with the land's natural beauty. According to the cemetery's history guide, the design was in the style of "rural" park cemeteries, then the fashion in New England. A rural park cemetery mimicked the English Romantic style of landscape design, including natural plantings, curved drives, and a picturesque setting—in this case, the water that would twice be artificially raised, thus leaving Evergreen Cemetery on an island in what is now known as Lake Menomin.

Knapp, Stout ran the cemetery for thirty years before turning it over to the city in 1904. Even then a company executive served as president of the new cemetery association into the mid-1930s.

In most respects the cemetery maintains its original design and appearance. In recent years, though, a handsome new stone entrance was built (using the same kind of Dunnville cutstone from nearby Downsville that the city's most prominent citizen, Andrew Tainter, used in construction of Menomonie's iconic Mabel Tainter Memorial Theater). The first sight for visitors is a statue of a Civil War soldier standing tall over a triangular plot dedicated to Civil War dead (there are also casualties of the Spanish-American War and later conflicts). Memorial Day activities have been held at the site since 1878.

Perhaps because it was a company-run cemetery, early records were kept in businesslike fashion, which allows today's searchers to know much about even the earliest residents of Evergreen. It is striking, Ohnstad said, to read how many of those in the cemetery's single-grave section died of causes such as infant cholera, diphtheria, scarlet fever, consumption, and typhoid fever. Young mothers died in childbirth and fathers in lumber mill accidents; there were suicides and mysterious deaths. Relatively few died of old age, which then was considered to be as young as sixty-five.

The history guide does not pull rank. It identifies the burial sites of such onetime citizens as Olaf Losby, who came from Norway to work in the store for Knapp, Stout and, later, in a downtown store. W. A. Scanlon operated Palace Livery Stables. Jacob Houss did hard and often-dangerous labor for Knapp, Stout, working spring log drives before he cleared land to farm and raise twelve children. Then there were the Voedisch sisters, daughters of the man who ran a funeral home and furniture business, and who were a popular singing duo in the region.

Fittingly for a cemetery built at the behest of lumber barons, there are noticeable monuments to the titans of timber and commerce. William Wilson, one of Menomonie's founders and one of Knapp, Stout's original owners, is remembered by a marker so massive that it had to be hauled over the ice by multiple teams of horses (stories vary: six teams, maybe more?) because it was too heavy to pull down the hill to the cemetery entrance. As if its size did not impart enough message about the man it remembers, the marker displays Wilson's likeness as well. Also here is James Huff Stout, the founder of what would become University of Wisconsin–Stout, who married Wilson's daughter, Angelina.

Many other prominent residents of early Menomonie are buried on the cemetery's highest elevation—"the hill," as it is called. There are the Knapps and Tainters. It was Andrew Tainter who had the Mabel Tainter Memorial built to honor the daughter who preceded him in death. Tainter apparently relocated some of his relatives, including his father, from other places to be with him for

Photo by Dennis McCann

Revolutionary War veteran Stephen Tainter is the only resident of Evergreen Cemetery with his own state historical marker.

the long haul. He also relocated Stephen Tainter, a Revolutionary War veteran who had served as drummer boy after his enlistment in Massachusetts in 1776. Stephen Tainter later reenlisted five times, serving with militias in six states, and after the war became a doctor, eventually moving to Prairie du Chien where in 1847 he died and was buried, if only temporarily. Thus Stephen Tainter, the only permanent resident of Evergreen with his own state historical marker to tell his story, is a man who never lived in the city.

Evergreen has come a long way from the days when, as Ohnstad put it, it was an extension of "the company store." But it clearly reflects those days, both in the conspicuous markers of prominent people and in the contemplative setting that its designers envisioned. The "Rural Romantic" design, she said, was a natural setting that offered a sanctuary, the better to "encourage reflection about one's own mortality."

It does that, just as it leaves a place of rest for everyone from the barons to poor Bye.

Photo by Mark Fay

Forest Home Cemetery, Milwaukee

The "Who Was Who" of Forest Home
Milwaukee

When I lived in Milwaukee some years back, I would often take out-of-town visitors to see the big-city sights. We'd rubberneck the fancy mansions along Lake Drive, stop at a Lake Michigan beach or two, perhaps take in a brewery tour or music festival. Of course we would ride through Forest Home Cemetery, which is a big city all by itself.

If any of the guests found that last stop morbidly strange, none said so. But had anyone questioned the choice, I would have had an answer: This place for the dead has always been a place for the living as well.

Forest Home has been a tourist stop from its earliest days, when thousands of people, many bearing picnic lunches, would travel by carriage or streetcar to spend summer Sundays on its bucolic grounds. As author John Gurda wrote in *Silent City*, his history of Forest Home's first one hundred and fifty years, the sprawling cemetery has long served not only as a place to bury the dead but also as arboretum and sculpture garden, nature preserve and museum of local history.

That last role is more than incidental. The cemetery is almost always referred to as "historic Forest Home," and both the cemetery and its handsome stone chapel are on the National Register of

Historic Places. Forest Home offers historic walking tours, both guided and self-guided, and in 1982 proudly opened a combination mausoleum and museum called The Halls of History; the former houses the crypts of those who chose aboveground interment over the traditional, while the latter space shares with visitors the life stories of the cemetery's—and by extension Milwaukee's—most famous residents.

Among Forest Home's "Who Was Who" are fifteen Milwaukee mayors, five Wisconsin governors, and enough generals to mount a sizable army. The beer barons who made Milwaukee famous are there, from Frederick Pabst, Jacob Best, and Joseph Schlitz to August Uihlein and Valentin Blatz, all buried under large markers that face each other in a section known as Brewers' Corner.

Milwaukee's captains of industry are there as well: William Davidson of Harley-Davidson, Lynde Bradley of Allen-Bradley, the banker Alexander Mitchell, Frederick Usinger of sausage fame, Henry Harnischfeger of heavy equipment, the tanner Guido Pfister and his partner Frederick Vogel, Edward Allis of Allis-Chalmers, the newspaperman Lucius Nieman, and on and on.

Billy Mitchell, the pilot-general often called the father of the U.S. Air Force, is there, as is Christopher Sholes, known as the inventor of the first practical typewriter. Even the arts are remembered, if somewhat immodestly. The monument at the graves of Alfred Lunt and Lynn Fontanne notes that they were "universally regarded as the greatest acting team in the history of the English speaking theatre."

But bit players in life's drama are present in far greater numbers, or, as Gurda put it, there are far more there who drank Schlitz and Pabst and Blatz than ever produced it. Since August 5, 1850, when one Oliver Cadwell earned the distinction of being Forest Home's first resident, more than one hundred thousand burials have taken place there, and still there is room for more.

The cemetery was organized by St. Paul's Episcopal Church in 1849 to serve the growing city's burial needs, or at least Protestants' burial needs. Catholics, Lutherans, and Jews would build their own

Photo by Mark Fay

The grave of Frederick Pabst, Forest Home Cemetery, Milwaukee

cemeteries, but none would match Forest Home's scale and historic status. The seventy-two-and-a-half-acre site was then several miles from the outskirts of town, but growth seemed inevitable. The land itself, sandy loam deemed most suitable for digging, offered the scenic and rolling setting for a cemetery that was to follow the "rural" or "garden" model made popular by Mount Auburn in Cambridge, Massachusetts. Making a cemetery a pleasant place to be and visit was a dramatic departure from the small churchyard cemeteries and scattered family plots that had been the norm.

Forest Home was surveyed and laid out by the decidedly famous scientist and naturalist Increase Lapham, who is buried there as well. The cemetery's interred population grew quickly. From two hundred burials in 1851, the cemetery came to hold twenty thousand by 1886 and thirty thousand by the turn of the century. It was such a pretty and peaceful place that the dead seldom lacked visitors.

"Whether they were lot-owners or not," Gurda wrote, "people simply couldn't get enough of the cemetery, particularly on Sunday—the week's only day of rest." By 1857 a private transit company began offering horse-drawn omnibus rides from downtown to Forest Home, followed later by horse-drawn streetcars and eventually a small, steam-powered locomotive, a grand bit of progress that also posed unique concerns. To prevent the little train from frightening horses on its way to the cemetery, the train's owners mounted a stuffed mule on the front of the engine as a disguise.

By 1888, a gatekeeper reported as many as eight thousand summer Sunday visitors. And what those observers found were the same visual wonders that greet visitors today: fountains and gardens and green space as well as enormous monuments and ornate examples of Victorian funerary architecture.

While the first burials lay beneath unremarkable stones, what might be called monument mania soon broke out. Real estate magnate Elisha Eldred's marble stone, installed in 1860, measured nineteen feet high and three feet on each side and weighed more than three tons. It wasn't the largest for long. One family marker weighed a whopping twenty tons, Gurda wrote, and in 1882, the widow of meatpacker D. C. Abbey commissioned a seventy-five-ton monster marker to remember her man.

The building boom led to soaring obelisks and mansion-esque mausoleums; at forty feet high, thirty feet wide, and weighing more than five hundred tons, brewer Valentin Blatz's mausoleum became the largest private structure in the cemetery. One tall stone honors the victims of the 1883 Newhall House fire, which destroyed one of the state's largest hotels and killed about 90 who were trapped inside, many of them young Irish maids. Yet most of the women the monument remembers are not buried there at all; the majority are buried in Catholic Calvary Cemetery, where a similar Newhall House monument also stands.

If the massive monuments are noteworthy and popular with visitors, some smaller markers are just as interesting: the train engine that remembers a railroad engineer, the firefighter's hat and hose on another stone, or the stack of marble books that holds the "Hood's Family Record," recording a family's lives and deaths on its jacket.

One of my personal favorites is the rather substantial casket-size monument that remembers Henry C. Payne—and which proves that he who pays for the stone can leave any message he desires.

The inscription warms up with, "In loving memory of Henry Clay Payne, sometime postmaster of the United States. Born November 23, 1843. Died October 4, 1904." Then it hits its stride: "An able executive. A public spirited citizen. A kindly neighbor. A loyal friend. A benefactor of the deserving. After life's fitful fever he sleeps well."

His wife, Lydia Wood Van Dyke, got a small marker that sits in front of her husband's. Her marker rises a few inches off the ground and says merely, "Wife of Henry Clay Payne. Asleep in Jesus."

The Talkative Cameron Tombstones
Little Prairie

The little corner cemetery in this little country town has a long-term resident notable enough to have earned his own historical marker, and while I had come for other reasons I stopped to read it. The side of the marker that faces the highway describes David Janes as a descendant of William Bradford III, the first governor of the Plymouth Colony, and notes that he enlisted in 1782 in Massachusetts to fight in the Revolutionary War.

I had to go into the cemetery to read the story on the marker's other side, where it explains further: Janes was discharged in 1783 and eventually moved to Wisconsin to live with his son. He died in Wisconsin in 1848 at age eighty-six and was buried in the Little Prairie cemetery.

To nitpick, the birth-death math on his marker added up to only eighty-five, but that's a small enough mystery to leave for another day. Besides, it was two other markers—one of them similarly bearing a two-sided narrative—that had brought me to this blink-and-you'll-miss-it crossroads near the Waukesha-Walworth county line. They are the Cameron tombstones, as chatty as grave markers get in these parts, yet for all they tell, they still leave the visitor wanting to know much more.

The newest marker is for John D. Cameron and reads, "Died September 21, 1946, in Chicago, Illinois, at age 80."

And then:

International Harvestore Company
Pension Certificate
This to certify that John D. Cameron upon retirement from active duty has been awarded a pension in recognition of long faithful and efficient service through a period of 41 years and one month.
This certificate is not transferable or assignable.
Dated at Chicago Illinois this fifteenth day of September 1931.
Alex Legge, President.

Cameron's is without question the only tombstone I have ever seen bearing witness to a man's pension.

But why? Was it simple pride, perhaps, that he had worked faithfully and efficiently for his employer all those years?

Was it a way of saying, well, maybe I can't take it with me, but I'll take it as far as I can?

Or did his widow have that inscribed as a way of saying thank you to International Harvestore—or to her husband—for not leaving her destitute?

Answers eluded me, so I moved a few feet to the marker for Duncan Cameron, who died March 20, 1922, also in Chicago, Illinois, age twenty-four.

Down the front side of his tall stone, his story follows:

James Wadsworth Grade School, Chi., Ill., 1911
Hyde Park High School, Chicago, Ill., 1915
Michigan University, Ann Arbor, Michigan, 1919
Received Degree of Bachelor of Arts

On the back of his stone was more:

Enrolled as
Boy Scout of America 1911
Member Delta Tau Delta Fraternity 1916
Life Member University of Michigan Union 1918

Member United States Naval Reserve Force 1918
Assistant Instructor in Navigation, University of Michigan 1918
Member University of Michigan Faculty
Special Assistant for War Courses in Electrical Engineering 1918
Assistant Manager University of Michigan Varsity Football Team 1918
Member the American Legion of Michigan 1918
Ervin Prieskonn Post Number 48
Griffins—University of Michigan All-Campus Society Elective 1919
Druids—University of Michigan Senior Literary Society Elective 1919
Endowment Member of Alumni Association of the University of Michigan 1920
Business Manager of The Michigansian, The Annual Yearbook of the University of Michigan, The XXIII Volume 1919

Quite a life for someone who lived to only twenty-four. A brass veteran's star showed he also had served in World War I, which completed the story of a short but fully lived life.

Still, there are so many questions unresolved.

If Duncan Cameron died in 1922, was his death somehow related to his war service—perhaps a lingering injury or the effects of gas? Why so much minutiae on the marker? Was working on the yearbook worth remembering for posterity? Did the stonecutter work so cheaply that Michigan could be written out every time instead of being abbreviated? Did his family, bereft at the loss of such a promising son, include every accomplishment they could in order to soften the blow of his death?

"What I tell myself," said Walworth County history writer Ginny Hall, who told me about the stones years ago, "they probably put all that down about Duncan because he was the first one in the family to go to college, and they were quite proud of it."

It is a good guess, but I still find it odd that the most informative stone in this or most other cemeteries should be such a head-scratcher.

When I first saw the stones some years ago I wrote them off as curiosities, but later I tried to learn a bit more about the mysterious Camerons. I called the president of the cemetery association, whose name was posted on a sign on the fence, but he didn't know the story. Nor did the former president, Dick Baker, but he was curious, too, and promised to make some calls and get back to me.

A week later he did, and then he followed up with an e-mail from Tom Rauschke of the Palmyra Historical Society. Rauschke included this account from the March 23, 1922, *Palmyra Enterprise*:

> The remains of Duncan Cameron of Chicago were brought here yesterday and taken to Little Prairie, where they were laid to rest after the burial service read by Rev. Knutzen. The young man was a victim of tuberculosis. He was the son of Mr. and Mrs. John Cameron, and was born 23 years ago while his parents lived at Little Prairie where his father kept store. He is survived by his wife and parents, all of whom were too ill to accompany the remains to this place. His uncle, James Cameron, came up with the body and was met here by Henry Coombe of Whitewater, and other relatives.

And so the mystery is at least partially explained. The family's loss was great, and so they honored their promising son by spelling out his short life on a stone marker that would long outlive the young man buried beneath it.

The pension, though. What do we make of that?

The Tombstone Tavern
Medford

It might have been a different story if farm fields had surrounded the little tavern. "Cornstalk Pizza" doesn't sound quite right.

But the bar owned in the 1960s by brothers Joseph "Pep" and Ronald Simek had other neighbors, and quiet ones at that. Across the street from their tavern was Evergreen Cemetery, which also owned the land next door. Another cemetery was an eighth of a mile up the road.

"We were surrounded by cemeteries," Pep Simek recalled years later, "so we named our place the Tombstone Tap."

One Sunday Pep was tending bar, and, because it was a Sunday after all, he had a few drinks while working. This was in the day when a glass of beer was ten cents and the "Peppermint Twist" was still too young to be an oldie; when the hot new song came on, Pep asked his wife to dance. Why don't you sit down before you fall down, she told him, but before he could sit Pep fell on some spilled beer underfoot, and in the process he broke his leg.

Stuck in the bar's small kitchen, he decided to make the best of his downtime. He started experimenting with pizza recipes, taking guidance from Chicago pizzas he had long enjoyed, and eventually he came up with what he thought was a winner—just the right spices, sauce, real Wisconsin cheese, and meats.

Customers thought it a winner, too, and couldn't get enough. Word spread, and before long other taverns were getting pizzas from the Tombstone Tap to serve to their own customers. Pep and Ron and their wives, Joan and Frances, began making pizzas by volume in the rooms attached to the Tap; the pizzas—by then they were referred to as Tombstones or Tombstone pizzas—were delivered in a 1959 Cadillac until the expanding business required purchase of its first refrigerated truck in 1966. Many expansions later, Tombstone's revenue surpassed $100 million.

In 1986 Kraft General Foods bought out the brothers, and the Tombstone brand became nationally known and sold. Pep wasn't too sure about the resulting changes. The product's early advertising stressed homespun themes, he said, calling Tombstone "the Italian pizza with a western name."

But Kraft ads headed in a different direction. In one notable TV spot, an executioner asked a condemned man, "What do you want on your Tombstone?"

"Cheese and pepperoni," the man replied.

"It worked out for Kraft," Pep said, though he still thought it an odd, well, twist, to use death row to sell pizzas.

And he may have a point. Even to a pizza man, "cheese and pepperoni" are hardly noble last words.

Photo by Mark Fay

Peter Cameron was Emma Eastman's fourth husband.

The Virgin Em and Her Many Husbands

McGregor, Iowa

The Eastman Cemetery is not on Wisconsin soil, but . . .

I was in Wisconsin, in a reading room at the La Crosse Public Library, when I came upon the story of Emma Eastman, a story so good I have no memory of my original mission that day. Much of Emma's colorful life and a number of her marriages played out in western Wisconsin. And the town of McGregor gets something of an asterisk on the issue of statehood, because it lies just across the wide Mississippi River from Wisconsin, within full view of our shore.

But enough rationalization. As men tended to be, I was smitten when I met Emma—luckily, decades too late to propose marriage—and I gave myself over that day to pursue her story.

She was known as "the Virgin Em," in the same way a big man can be called Tiny or a milquetoast answer to Butch. This was, after all, a woman who was buried with three husbands near at hand, and who had six more sprinkled through her past. If Elizabeth Taylor was an optimist every time she walked down the aisle she still couldn't hold a candle to Emma Eastman.

That much I learned that winter day in the library from writer Myer Katz's *Echoes of Our Past*, his history of La Crosse that included an account of "the beautiful and incredible Emma Cameron," as she was known in her La Crosse days. The surname came from her marriage to Peter Cameron, in the city's very first wedding. Of course, it was Emma's fourth and far from last. (Later in her life, Emma was said to have lamented she had not made it "an even dozen.")

Well, when I read further that Emma was buried an hour downriver in McGregor—in "a queer necropolis" with six of her former husbands (he was wrong on the number but not the main point)—I couldn't go home without heading first to McGregor to find that boneyard.

The various accounts of Emma's life and loves differ on details—and some go out of their way to adorn the tale with wild charges, as if a pistol-packing pioneer woman with nine husbands needs any help—but a former McGregor man, Ronald G. Harris, has spent much time tracking down public records that tell Emma's story.

According to Harris's book, *Eastman Cemetery*, Emma was born in Ohio in 1823 to Peter and Mary Coleman Eastman, who would move to western Wisconsin and then cross the river to McGregor in 1838. A year earlier, at just fourteen, Emma had married Ephraim Kellogg. The union did not last. Nor did her 1839 marriage in Grant County, Wisconsin, to a man who soon divorced her on the basis of her subsequent marriage to yet another man, named Cunningham, that same year. (There is more evidence of marriage in her life than divorce; Emma apparently found it easier to just move on than to deal with legal niceties.)

Her capacity for finding husbands might have grown out of what one account called her "unsurpassingly beautiful figure and features, remarkable nerve (and) great presence of mind . . . ," or, more likely, from her "capacity to model one of the opposite sex to her wishes as readily and gently as an artist molds a figure in plastic."

Whatever the case, Peter Daniel Cameron signed on as husband number four in 1846, telling his family in a later letter, "I got myself a wife sometime since," according to Harris. By other accounts Emma was a prominent character in early La Crosse social life. She was said to ride horseback through town, carrying a rifle. She was also said to have possessed a notable temper but apparently could be diplomatic as well; one report said she helped avert an Indian attack through her knowledge of the Indian language.

In 1849 Peter killed a man in a dispute over ownership of logs and was jailed in Prairie du Chien. He was released some years later. After his death in 1854, Emma was drawn into a lengthy court fight over control of his property; Harris wrote that her fifth husband, Ralph C. Bowles, helped her with the property disputes. Emma didn't need help the night Peter's brother, Daniel, went to her house to attempt to recover some deeds. Emma pulled a pistol from under her pillow and fired two shots, leaving Daniel with a hole in his coat and a piece of his little finger gone.

Emma was not charged, and, in an ad in a local newspaper, she claimed self-defense. "I have no remorse of conscience in defending my own life in my own house, and in the dark in the absence of my husband," she wrote. "My fore fathers fought in the Revolutionary War for their freedom and rights, and I hope their grand-daughter, Emma C. Bowles, has too noble a heart to let one Scotch Tory rob her."

Alas, later that same year Emma petitioned for divorce from Ralph, entering into the court record a letter he had mailed from Missouri accusing her of adultery, including his inclination to look her up and hang her except that it would "nasty up a perfectly good rope."

Emma next entered into sacred union with Nelson Sharp in Prairie du Chien in 1861 and, after his death, in 1863 married DeWitt Clinton Van Sickle, a man she called Clinty. Harris writes that, after Van Sickle died behind a team of runaway horses in 1881 (what, you expected natural causes?), Emma had a grave marker made that read:

"Clinty, my heart clings to thee, love. In heaven I hope to meet above. You was ever kind and true to me. So was I to you. Emma C. V."

Photo by Mark Fay

This stone (far right) replaced DeWitt Clinton Van Sickle's original headstone.

Van Sickle was buried in Eastman Cemetery, along with other family members that included Emma's sister Anna, her father, and, later, her sister Louisa. According to Harris, the WPA Cemetery Recording Project lists husband number eight, Michael Stence, as also being buried in Eastman Cemetery. So was her last husband, Joseph A. Wilson, who survived her.

Nevertheless, as I approached the town of McGregor that day and my first stop at the public library, I wondered just how much was apocryphal and how I would find the little cemetery where Emma lay at rest. Was anyone else even aware of the Virgin Em?

The answer was yes. I no more than said her name when library director Michele Pettit pointed over my shoulder to a wall mural of McGregor scenes, including one depicting Emma in a black dress, standing in front of her husbands' graves with a flower in her hand and a tear tracing down her cheek, and handed me a flier for an upcoming Valentine's Day program on "The Many Loves of Emma Eastman," featuring Pat Matt of nearby Elkader as Emma.

Best of all, Pettit gave me directions to Eastman Cemetery: out of town and into the country a ways to Keystone Road, then down the driveway to the Milewsky farm, where a small sign pointed to the cemetery on a wind-whipped hill. Many of the original stones had long since disappeared, but a few years earlier a Scout troop and members of the Clayton County Pioneer Cemetery Restoration Commission had worked to renovate Eastman Cemetery, clearing brush and weeds and scrub trees. It is believed about thirty graves are on the site (including a more recent stone for Van Sickle), which is protected by a chain fence and has a welcoming arch that reads "Eastman."

Later, I called Harris in Wisconsin Rapids to talk about Emma. He spoke of the challenge of separating fact from fiction in her story, and why he was so determined to do so.

"The reason she is so intriguing is, I don't know what she would be called now, a schizophrenic or something," he said, citing tales of her fiery temper. "She apparently was a beautiful woman, too.

"I think now I like her as kind of a character," Harris continued. "If I had known her I probably would have disliked her."

Or married her. It's what men did.

Wisconsin's Smallest Man
Ixonia

It is dangerous to accept biggest-tallest-smallest-widest or any other superlative at face value, but John Lewis's claim to fame is etched in granite on a country hillside in the cemetery of the long-gone Welsh Presbyterian Church.

And if something is etched on a cemetery stone, how could it not be true?

The stone names his parents and their birth and death dates, but the particulars on John Lewis are the eye-catchers.

> *Born Oct. 10, 1856. Died March 21, 1881, at the age of twenty-four. Weight 19 pounds. 27 inches high. The smallest man on record.*

That's a claim to stop the most casual cemetery stroller in his tracks.

Lewis was born in Ixonia, in Jefferson County, and died there. His parents—his father was named Lewis Lewis, his mother Catherine—were natives of Wales whose union produced seven children. Only John, who also lacked thumbs and had a club foot, was of unusual size. He was so small that the famous Tom Thumb, at forty inches tall, towered over him when they eventually—maybe inevitably—met.

Lewis—or, as a Milwaukee newspaper inelegantly put it on the occasion of his death, "the Ixonia dwarf"—had a taste for stylish dress. The paper said he favored a blue frock with brass buttons and a hat, made expressly for his small head, which made him look "like a miniature Broadway swell." He was said to have been bright, fluent in both English and Welsh, and able to recite the New Testament by heart. He often led the traditional hymn singing at Ixonia Welsh Methodist Church.

Unlike Tom Thumb and another famous carnival draw, the tiny Commodore Nutt, Lewis never subjected himself to public exhibition or otherwise exploited his small size. P. T. Barnum was said to have recruited Lewis, but his mother was adamant that he not leave home, especially not to be exhibited, and in the end his most distant travel was to Oshkosh for a church convention.

Still, when Tom Thumb and the Commodore were in the area, Lewis went to see them, the paper said. And if it was awkward for the three of them, imagine what a scene it must have been for other witnesses.

"All three of these men midgets were greatly interested in each other," the paper said. "Nutt admitted he was beat, but pointed to Lewis' hands and foot as an offset for over-height. Thumb had almost nothing to say, being almost a giant compared with the Ixonia specimen of humanity."

Such florid writing aside, it is a curious notion to think of Tom Thumb looking down on another man.

Lewis died at twenty-four after a bout of stomach congestion, just months after casting his first presidential ballot. At least he cast it for a winner.

"From this it will be seen that General Garfield had not only the largest support," the paper noted, "but the smallest supporter in the country."

Belle Boyd, Confederate Spy

Wisconsin Dells

Spring Grove Cemetery, a rare place of peace and quiet amidst the honky-tonk that is today's Wisconsin Dells, is the resting place of not only the man who put this tourist town on the map but a woman whose own feisty fame is worth recalling.

H. H. Bennett was the legendary photographer of the still-wild Wisconsin River, the singular geography of the region, and the faces of its Native American residents. His early stereoscopic images helped lure the first tourists to the area in the years after the Civil War. Bennett is buried beneath an impressive stone on a small rise in Spring Grove, though nothing calls special attention to the grave of the man who drew the world's attention to the Dells.

The same cannot be said of another nearby grave, larger and more ornate than most of those around it. The burial site of Belle Boyd is covered with a concrete slab and set off by a metal fence; if that's not enough to draw the wanderer's eye, a little flag of the Confederate States blows in the breeze, the symbol of Southern defiance in the heart of the Union North.

Her marker reads: "Confederate Spy. Born in Virginia. Died in Wisconsin. Erected by a comrade."

As you can guess, there is more to the story.

She was, by name and nature, a true Southern belle. Born in

Martinsburg, in what is now West Virginia, seventeen-year-old Belle Boyd rallied to the cause when the South announced its secession from the Union but was denied by her gender the opportunity to carry a weapon and fight.

Nevertheless, Boyd found a way to fight the North, though in only one instance did she use a weapon. When drunken Union soldiers entered her family's home and attempted to raise their flag in place of the Confederate flag, an irate Boyd—"my indignation was aroused beyond control," she later said—shot one of them dead with a pistol.

More often, though, her weapons were her womanly wiles. By various accounts Boyd was not beautiful in the classic sense (though one assessment did give her "the best pair of legs in the Confederacy") but possessed a charm and power over men—even, or maybe especially, Northern officers. And when she put her power to use in enticing Northern officers to share secrets that could help the South, Boyd became a valuable spy. On one occasion, she picked up Northern strategy by hiding inside a closet over a dining room where officers were meeting; Boyd listened through a knothole and then relayed the news to Confederate forces. More famously, she once ran from a hotel to the camp of General Stonewall Jackson, braving gunfire as she crossed open fields in her blue calico dress, and waved her sunbonnet as a signal for Jackson to advance.

Boyd was jailed on several occasions, though at least once a kindly general released her. While imprisoned in Washington, Boyd drew attention for singing Southern songs through the barred windows. She was captured again while en route to Europe, but so sympathetic was one of her captors that he became her first of three husbands. Curiously, all were Northerners.

Boyd emerged from the war with a fame she continued to exploit. Her book about her spy days, *Belle Boyd in Camp and Prison*, was a popular seller. Boyd later traveled extensively throughout the country speaking and performing, but by then it was in favor of national unity. Her new message was, "One God, one people, one flag, forever." It was on such a tour in June 1900 that Boyd, after appearances in Portage and Pardeeville, arrived in today's Wisconsin Dells, then called Kilbourn, where she suffered a heart attack and died.

Her burial in Spring Grove was more a matter of convenience than geography, and had she died in Pardeeville or Portage Belle Boyd might have passed quietly into history. But the Dells, ever alert to promotional opportunities, saw an edge in her presence. In the early 1950s a small group of men tidied up Boyd's grave, in part to call attention and attract tourists, and held a parade. About that time a Dells tour boat was christened the *Belle Boyd*, which made more people aware of her past and of her presence. The governor of Virginia sent flags for Boyd's grave to the governor of Wisconsin, who, for lack of a better plan, sent them to the American Legion post in the Dells.

There, Oliver Reese of the American Legion agreed to raise the Confederate flag, the flag of the commonwealth of Virginia, and the American flag at Boyd's grave on Memorial Day. The next year, he returned and did it again.

"I thought maybe I'd get relieved sometime," he said a few years ago, "but nobody volunteered."

So Reese, who coincidentally was married to H. H. Bennett's granddaughter Jean, handled the honors for fifty years. In 2004, he raised the flags for the last time before handing off the duty to his daughter and her husband. Reese's service did not go unappreciated. To thank him for his contribution to the memory of Belle Boyd—and the Confederacy—members of the Elliott Grays Chapter of the United Daughters of the Confederacy (UDC) traveled to Wisconsin to watch Reese raise the flags one last time. They carried with them a letter of thanks from the governor of Virginia, a certificate of thanks from the Daughters' Virginia division president, and the UDC Stonewall Jackson Medal to present to Reese.

"It's the first time our chapter has awarded the medal," Ruth Snead of Richmond told me at the time.

And it went to a Northerner!

What impressed Reese even more was that the Elliott Grays Chapter, deciding turnabout was in order, agreed to place a wreath at the Wisconsin Union Monument on Pole Green Road in Mechanicsville, Virginia, honoring the men of the Thirty-sixth Wisconsin Volunteer Infantry who were killed or wounded in battle there on June 1, 1864.

Of course, the Dells again took advantage and turned the visit by the Daughters into an opportunity to promote the area. Chapter members and their husbands were guests at the American Legion Memorial Day picnic in Bowman Park and treated to a tour of the H. H. Bennett Museum and of the Jennie Bowman House, which is home to chairs made by Confederate president Jefferson Davis.

And, as you knew they would be, the group was taken on a boat tour of the scenic Upper Dells. Their boat was an apt choice, because it had been christened by Elliott Grays Chapter president Mrs. J. W. Phillips in 1952, using waters from the James River in Virginia. It was, of course, the *Belle Boyd*.

The Lake Superior Surfer
Washburn

In a sun-drenched hillside cemetery overlooking Lake Superior is the latest exhibit in my so far one-man campaign for more revealing headstones.

Here is what the marker tells you: "Thomas E. Blake, U.S. Coast Guard, WWII, died in 1994."

Here is what it doesn't even hint: that Tom Blake of little Washburn grew up to be one of the world's great ocean surfers, an innovator and inventor, in beach circles a wave-riding legend on the order of the great Hawaiian Duke Kahanamoku himself.

Who was, as it happens, Blake's close friend.

Blake also served as stunt double for Johnny Weismuller, Clark Gable, and other stars of the silver screen, and his swimming skills put him in two halls of fame.

Not bad for a boy whose first icy waves spilled out of Lake Superior.

What isn't recorded on Blake's stone is told in a small exhibit at the Washburn Historical Museum and collected in a book called *Tom Blake Surfing 1922–32*, written by Gary Lynch, former historian for *Surfer Magazine*. According to Lynch, Blake was born in 1902 and grew up in Washburn, where he was educated until 1918, when schools closed due to the Spanish influenza epidemic.

Though still a teenager, Blake traveled around looking for work, a search that led him in 1920 to Detroit and a chance encounter with the legendary swimmer and surfer Duke Kahanamoku, an Olympic gold medalist Blake had admired since watching a newsreel clip of surfboarding Hawaiians as a youth. Inspired by the Duke, Blake headed west to pursue swimming in southern California. There he received a few lessons in basic skills at the Santa Monica beach from Kahanamoku himself.

Blake supported himself with lifeguard work, but he also persuaded a night watchman at the Los Angeles Athletic Club to let him train in the club's pool for the swimming races that might also provide him with a little income. Less than a year later, Blake won the grueling Amateur Athletic Union's National Ten-Mile Open in the frigid Delaware River at Philadelphia, which gave him a major boost in his new career. For the next seven years he competed in swimming events while continuing to work as a lifeguard and as a body double and stuntman in dozens of watery films.

The magic of movie making did not impress him much. Speaking later about his work in the movie *When the Pavement Ends*, Blake said, "Working in films was always a trade-off for food and shelter. They made me wrestle with a dead shark in that film."

As the many photos in Lynch's book indicate, Blake was blessed with good looks, but he was gifted with smarts as well. After 1930 he began tinkering with photography, eventually moving to self-portraits of his own athletic figure (he was always careful about his diet) clad in racy swim trunks and occasionally less. He built the first waterproof camera housing used in surf photography, producing images for his own book on surfing and eventually for *National Geographic*.

In 1924 Blake traveled for the first time to Hawaii, where, as champion swimmer and friend of the Duke, he was warmly received. He was, literally and figuratively, a world away from little Washburn.

"I sat at their luaus, watched their most beautiful women dance the hulas," he later said. "I was invited into their exclusive Hui Nalu surfriding club, at the time a club for natives only. I have held the honor position (bow seat) riding waves in the outrigger canoe and . . . was initiated into the secrets of spearfishing far out on the coral reefs."

The islands fit his nature—"it is life's compensation for such a nature as mine," he later said—and he reveled in their culture. At the Bishop Museum in Honolulu, he marveled at huge Olo surfboards and was granted permission to restore them, learning in the process secrets of board design that he would refine through the years. He made his own boards with air chambers and was honored when Duke Kahanamoku built a hollow sixteen-foot board of Blake's design.

Blake, Lynch wrote, was the only man other than his famous friend the Duke to be inducted into both Florida's Swimming Hall of Fame and California's International Surfing Hall of Fame. Yet although Blake was a champion surfer in his own right—in 1928 he won the first Pacific Coast Surfing Championship—he said later that "to have been a surfing companion of the Duke in his prime was a privilege accorded to me. To see Duke coming in at Waikiki on his long Olo board was to see surfriding at its best. Somehow, to me, Duke is the last of the great Hawaiians, the man by which to measure the race, the surfrider by which to measure the surfriders of all time."

But as surfing companions faded away Blake's affection for Hawaii eventually waned. In 1955 he returned to the mainland.

"Tom Blake, one of Waikiki Beach's most familiar figures, left the Islands last night after admitting his 30-year romance with the white crescent of sand is over," the *Honolulu Star Bulletin* wrote. "The beauty of the surf, sand and sun never will die for him, he said, but the thrill of surfing that sparked the love affair is gone."

"I'm too old now, I guess," Blake told the paper with a sad smile. "I'm no longer happy here."

Eventually he returned to Washburn and lived just blocks from the big water he had known as a youth, continuing what he called his "communion with nature, under the blessed church of the open sky."

The Washburn Historical Museum's exhibit includes some of Blake's late-life philosophy. On the importance of education he wrote, "The knowledge you get in schools and colleges is second-hand. The wisdom and know-how you get from the sea and waves and water is vigor, new and fleeting. By all means get some of that education."

Lynch, the surfing historian, wrote, "A dozen or so other men might have eventually done everything Blake did singularly."

That would have been a nice addition to Blake's marker—that and a nod to the sea and waves and water that gave him life. A name and dates etched on stone, while truthful, miss a story as big as the greatest wave.

Heisman's Trophy
Rhinelander

Each December, as the college game evolves from handing off footballs to handing out awards, two questions arise, at least among a small number in Wisconsin:

Who will win the Heisman Memorial Trophy, widely viewed as designating the single best college player in the land?

And will that player finally be the one Heisman Trophy winner to visit the man for whom the award is named?

The answer to the first changes from year to year.

The answer to the second never varies. If the winners of the Heisman Trophy even know Heisman's first name or why the trophy carries his last, not one seems to have found his way to Rhinelander's Forest Home Cemetery to pay respects to one of early college football's true giants, who since 1936 has been at rest in his wife's family plot in northern Wisconsin.

It could be argued, from a partisan Wisconsin perspective, that Heisman is not the only deservingly famous person in Forest Home. Also buried there is Eugene Shepard, the legendary northwoods prankster who once rigged a jumping wooden fish to lure guests to his resort and whose most famous hoax was the "capture" of the first live hodag, the mythical lumbering-era beast. Rhinelander still has a Hodag Park and a statue of a snarling, menacing hodag at the city's visitor center, and high school sports teams wear the hodag name to this day. Truly, Shepard left his mark.

But for Richard Winquist, who served as sexton at Forest Home for thirty-two years until his retirement in 2003, Eugene Shepard's hodag can't touch John Heisman's trophy.

"My dad was there for twenty years before me," Winquist said, "and he used to say [Heisman's grave is] our one claim to fame."

It's no small claim, even if one Heisman winner in the 1960s was so moved by the honor as to ask, "The award is wonderful, but who's Heisman?"

John Heisman was born in Cleveland in 1869, two weeks before the first college football game was played between Princeton and Rutgers, and he played football as a youth and during his college years. Even after earning a law degree, Heisman stayed in the game as coach at Oberlin College, where his team went undefeated, and later at a

Photo by Dennis McCann

Few realize that football great John Heisman is buried in Rhinelander, Wis.

number of other colleges. There are few accounts of his career that don't refer to him as a pioneering coach and relentless innovator.

Heisman helped push the legalization of the forward pass in the early 1900s, a move he believed would open up the field and reduce the sometimes deadly—literally, in those early pad-free days—violence involved in stopping the ground game. He introduced the "hike" signal, pushed to divide the game into four quarters, developed the center snap, invented the hidden ball trick, and, in a fan-friendly gesture, started the use of scoreboards.

"Without John Heisman," said one *New York Times* profile a few years ago, "there might not be a forward pass in football, and without a forward pass, the game would probably have died from disinterest or been abolished because of its fatal brutality."

In his own coaching, Heisman stressed fundamentals—and a bit of high drama. When addressing his team, it's said, he would hold the ball in the air and say, "Better to have died as a small boy than to fumble this football." And, in a preview to current times, he was among the first college football coaches to rile faculty members by drawing an annual salary higher than any professor's.

After thirty-six years of coaching he retired to New York City, where he soon became athletic director of the new Downtown Athletic Club. Five years later, in 1935, the club began awarding a trophy to the best college player in the land. After Heisman's death in 1936, the award was renamed the Heisman Memorial Trophy.

It surprises some that the grave site of Heisman and his wife, Edith, is so modest: just a simple name-and-date ground-flush marker for each. When I went to visit one autumn I had to ask Marv Schumacher, who was tending to flowers in the cemetery, for help in finding it.

"I get that question a lot," he said as we walked to the grave. Maybe some visitors who know of Heisman's presence there expect to find a stone in the shape of the Heisman Trophy, or even a marker with a football player striking the iconic Heisman pose, which would be rather cool. But no.

"It's a rather insignificant [marker]," Schumacher said. "This famous man and just a ground-level stone. I wonder how many people know he's got a simple gravestone in Rhinelander, Wisconsin?"

Certainly some know, if only as a curiosity. Winquist, too, has guided visitors through the years. A few hard-core football fans come at all times of the year, but attention peaks in December, when the annual award ceremony is held in New York. Perhaps Wisconsinites paid the most attention the year the University of Wisconsin's popular running back Ron Dayne won the coveted trophy.

"There were rumors that Ron Dayne would come up [to visit the grave]," Winquist said, "but it was just rumors."

Yet Heisman is not ignored in Rhinelander. At the local airport, a memorial includes a list of all trophy winners and a wood bust of Heisman created by local art teacher Bob Kanyusik. A meeting room at a local motel is named for him as well. But that's not enough for everyone. More than twenty years ago an unknown visitor placed four tickets to a Minnesota Gophers football game in a jar, left it on the grave, and later wrote anonymously to the local paper suggesting the community do more to promote Heisman.

Heisman, of course, could not use the tickets. Winquist took the jar with him when he left his cemetery job, fearing his replacements would not understand its historical significance, and still has the jar and tickets in his basement rec room, souvenirs of a game not attended but tangible connections to Forest Home's most famous resident.

14

Poor Percival the Poet

Hazel Green

In the southwesternmost corner of the state, not far from where Wisconsin bumps against Iowa and Illinois, a historical marker points from the highway to a shaded little cemetery where history and melancholy serve as a tourist draw.

I'd been there before, because historic markers are not to be denied. Who would not be curious enough to stop and see whose life merited such a sign? But when I returned a few years ago to the grave of James Gates Percival it was with a higher mission than mere curiosity. I had recently noticed that the 150th anniversary of Percival's death and burial in Hazel Green was approaching, and while he was a lot of things in life—geologist, physician, linguist, and, most notably, the most famous poet you have never heard of—in death he has been mostly ignored.

"Few in the present generation," wrote Wisconsin historian Fred L. Holmes, "have heard of James Gates Percival."

And that was back in 1922. Lonely and melancholy in life, forgotten in death—that was Percival's fate. As one who makes a living by words, I thought it only proper to pay a visit to the late linguist in the anniversary year of his passing, so I found again the little cemetery near the corner of Church and Fairplay, where the highway sign points. Maybe I should have brought a Webster's dictionary to the grave and looked up a new word in his honor. A guide to Wisconsin rocks might have been nice, but I hadn't thought of that, either. I did bring some of his poems, but I felt a little funny about standing in a small-town cemetery reading verse aloud.

Percival might have understood my unease. He was by most accounts a genius, with all the eccentricities that so often come with that job. The marker in the cemetery gives some of his particulars: born in Connecticut in 1795, a graduate of Yale at twenty, then service as Connecticut's state geologist and, later, Wisconsin's first geologist.

But a lot was left out. He was said to have mastered a book on elementary astronomy at age five, and at fourteen to have composed his first epic poem. He was head of his class at Yale, was fluent in as many as ten languages, was licensed to practice medicine (but did not), studied botany, worked for a time in the 1820s with Noah Webster compiling a certain dictionary you may have heard about, produced books of poetry, and, for a short time, served as professor of chemistry at the U.S. Military Academy.

No underachiever, our Percy.

After geology became his favored work, he moved to Wisconsin and settled in Hazel Green, which was so much a part of the lead region that it was originally called Hard Scrabble, and more's the pity that name was lost. But while Percival found a home there, it can never be said that Percival found happiness. In any account of his life the word *melancholy* appears, often followed by *morbid*. A remembrance of Percival in the *Madison Democrat* in 1920 blamed lost love, saying, "It is believed that his spirit was blighted by a crushed affection in his young manhood. Disappointed in love, nature became his mistress."

But his melancholia may have set in earlier than that. One of his earliest poems was "The Suicide," which he later explained was "intended as a picture of the horror and wretchedness of a youth ruined by early perversion, and of the causes of that diversion. It is not without a moral to those who can see it."

So, whether from boyhood or early manhood, poor Percival

was a miserable wretch. In a profile, Henry Eduard Legler said, "with the exception of Edgar Allan Poe, no American poet has a life story so charged with the elements that evoke intense pity . . .

"[Percival] sought to end his life at age 25, and his poem on the subject of suicide embodies the train of thought that furnished the motive," Legler wrote. "He lived to be 60 years of age, and the publication of his first book was the one brief period of the three score years which seemed to him worth the living. Female companionship he sought once, and ever after avoided almost frantically; comradeship he repelled; companionship, except that of books, he avoided."

When Percival built his house, Legler wrote, it had no front door or windows.

Well, I thought, this should be quite an anniversary party. Overlooked as he usually is, however, at least in Hazel Green Percival is remembered. The main drag is called Percival Street, and for a while a local bed-and-breakfast was called Percival Country Inn. And there is that highway sign directing poetic spirits to his grave site, where the marker was the gift of a former Yale classmate who had learned that the noted poet was in an unmarked grave and had collected five hundred dollars to remedy the slight.

It reads: "Eminent as a Poet, Rarely Accomplished as a Linguist, Learned and acute in Science, A man without Guile."

I should have read a poem, however it might have looked. Maybe this, from his poem "Evening":

"Night steals on; and the day takes its farewell, like the words of a departing friend, or the last tone of hallowed music in a minister's aisles, heard when it floats along the shade of elms, in the still place of graves."

How melancholy. And how perfect.

Fort Crawford's Old Bones
Prairie du Chien

This rustic city on the banks of the Mississippi River was one of the first settlements in the territory that would become Wisconsin, so one would expect it to have old burial grounds.

And so it does—several of them. The first burial at Old French Cemetery on Frenchtown Road was in 1817. Father Lucien Galtier, whose chapel of St. Paul, Minnesota, gave that future twin city its name, is buried along with other early Catholics at St. Gabriel Church cemetery, which dates to the 1820s. Many of the founders of modern Prairie du Chien are interred at Evergreen Cemetery, which was set aside for that purpose in the 1840s.

Still, it is another old cemetery, not much bigger than a side yard, that might make a claim for the most historic burial yard. Fort Crawford Cemetery Soldiers Lot dates to the region's earliest days, back when such important historical figures as the young Jefferson Davis, the future president Zachary Taylor, and the ill-fated Indian leader Black Hawk were leaving footprints in the area around Prairie du Chien.

In the years after the War of 1812, Americans saw a need to establish a military presence along the Mississippi River, and so they built Fort Crawford, named for the then secretary of war William H. Crawford, on the site of the former Fort Shelby. The government failed to fully investigate the location, however, and the log fort flooded every few years until the commanding officer finally received permission to buy land on higher ground for another Fort Crawford.

Significant events occurred regularly at Prairie du Chien, one of Wisconsin's earliest communities, in the years before statehood. Indian treaties were signed in 1825, 1829, and 1830. In 1827 the Ho-Chunk leader Red Bird and a few followers killed several settlers and set off an "Indian scare" that led to Red Bird's surrender and imprisonment at Prairie du Chien.

Dr. William Beaumont's numerous experiments at Fort Crawford were credited with greatly advancing the medical understanding of digestion, research that is still celebrated at the Fort Crawford Museum on Beaumont Street. And during the Black Hawk War in the summer of 1832, a defeated Black Hawk surrendered to Colonel Zachary Taylor at the second Fort Crawford, where he was imprisoned for several days before he was transferred to St. Louis in the company of Lieutenant Jefferson Davis.

Fort Crawford was closed in 1856, but the small cemetery that sits midblock on Beaumont Street remains. The first burials were of officers stationed at Fort Crawford; later, family members and other enlisted soldiers were buried there as well. Of the sixty-four interments, nearly two-thirds of the markers read "Unknown Soldier."

Some stories are known, though. The first burial at Fort Crawford was for Lieutenant John Mackenzie, who was killed by a drunken soldier in 1828, and nearby is the grave of Colonel Willoughby Morgan, who spent his career on the Western frontier. As testament to the harsh conditions that prevailed in early Prairie du Chien, several of the graves house young women, many still in their teens at the time of their deaths, who were married to officers at Fort Crawford. A handful of large rectangular markers cover the graves of officers and their families.

The United States received title to the cemetery in 1866. While it falls under the umbrella of the U.S. Department of Veterans Affairs, Fort Crawford is deemed a soldier's lot as opposed to a national cemetery. Nevertheless, various news accounts and even penny postcards through the years have incorrectly called it the country's smallest national cemetery.

In the 1930s the United Daughters of the Confederacy erected a Jefferson Davis monument near the entrance to the soldier's lot, noting the brief service there of the future president of the Confederate States of America. Fort Crawford was also where Davis's romance with Zachary Taylor's daughter was thought to have been sparked.

In addition to Fort Crawford and the fifty-acre Wood National Cemetery in Milwaukee, where more than thirty-eight thousand burials have taken place, there are four other such "soldier's lots" in the state, including small sections at Forest Home Cemetery in Milwaukee, Forest Hill in Madison, Mound Cemetery in Racine, and Fort Winnebago Cemetery in Portage.

The story of the last is nearly identical to the story of Fort Crawford. Fort Winnebago Cemetery Soldier's Lot is near the site of Old Fort Winnebago, which was established in 1828 as one of a series of forts along the Fox-Wisconsin waterway that served as a transportation route between the Mississippi River and Lake Michigan. (Jefferson Davis served there, as well.)

The fort was closed in 1853 and the property sold, but the cemetery that had been established in 1835 was omitted from the deed. By default the United States retained the post cemetery, which was designated as a soldier's lot in 1862. There are seventy-five grave sites in the lot, including dead from the Revolutionary War, the War of 1812, the Civil War, the Spanish-American War, and World War I.

In 1924 the Wau-Bun chapter of the Daughters of the American Revolution erected a granite marker at Fort Winnebago dedicated to the memory of unknown dead.

But if Fort Crawford's story is all in the past, the little soldier's lot that survives it still has occasional life. Each Memorial Day the city holds traditional remembrance ceremonies there; local Girl Scouts adorn the graves with flowers, while Boy Scouts set up chairs and otherwise assist.

"It continues to be a site of gatherance, I guess you could say, for the community," said Don Ruehlow, who helps care for the soldier's lot. "And a lot of tourists make this one of their stops. There's a lot of interest and a lot of traffic there.

"The community here is very proud of this cemetery. They look at this cemetery as a jewel and not [just] as a cemetery stuck in the middle of town."

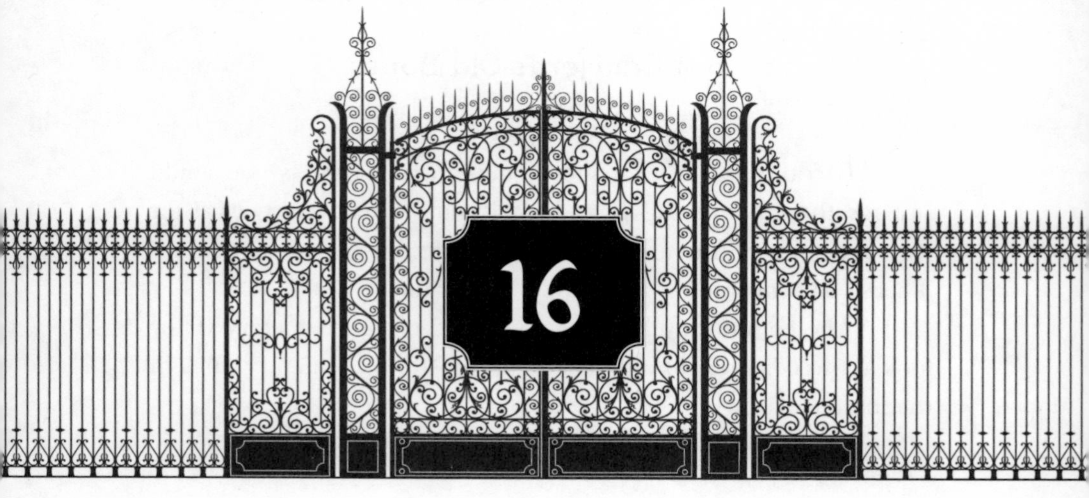

Confederates at Rest
Madison

In the bucolic 140-acre city park that is Forest Hill Cemetery, the most prominent names of state government and the great state university jump off of oversized stones.

This is as much a history park as a burying place.

Figures whose names grace tall stone buildings on the University of Wisconsin campus—Vilas and Van Hise, Birge and Steenbock—also grace headstones in Forest Hill. Frederick Jackson Turner, the great frontier historian and UW professor, is there as well, among other giants of higher learning.

At least eight former governors call Forest Hill their eternal home, most famously Robert M. "Fighting Bob" La Follette, his wife Belle, and a number of their family members. Louis Powell Harvey, the sitting governor who gave his life while delivering much-needed medical supplies to Wisconsin troops in the Civil War in 1862, is remembered with a granite marker, as is his wife Cordelia, who after her husband's untimely death became known as "the angel of Wisconsin" for her work to establish a national hospital system for soldiers.

Fittingly, just a long stone's throw from the Harveys' marker is a section for Union soldiers from that calamitous conflict. Tidy rows of soldiers' stones stand in rigid formation, just as the soldiers themselves once did.

Confederates at Rest

Many Wisconsin cemeteries have Civil War dead. What separates Forest Hill from almost any other is another soldiers' section just up the road from the Union dead, where a sign in front of approximately 140 similarly tidy soldiers' markers reads "Confederate Rest."

Absolutes are always dangerous, but one might safely say that this is the only cemetery anywhere containing both Indian mounds and Confederate soldiers. How did these Southern soldiers end up spending eternity so far from home? To understand, we turn toward the university down the road.

Think football.

In 1862, long before Camp Randall Stadium became Wisconsin's autumn weekend football palace, Camp Randall was a military camp for Union soldiers, a training ground for Wisconsin troops on the site of the former state fair grounds. It was named for then-governor Alexander W. Randall, and in the spring of that year the training facility took on an added mission—as prisoner-of-war camp.

That service was relatively short—just three months—and the number of captured Southern soldiers was never as high as at more prominent—some say more notorious—prisons such as Camp Douglas in Chicago. But in April 1862, Camp Randall became temporary home to some 880 Southerners, followed by another 300 a few days later.

Most of the captured Rebels were members of the First Regiment of Alabama Infantry, but there were members of units from Tennessee, Mississippi, and other states as well. And many were seriously ill, even dying, before their arrival in Madison. They had been involved in trying to keep control of the Mississippi River between Cairo, Illinois, and New Madrid, Missouri, and in the course of fighting had suffered wet, cold conditions that left many with chronic diarrhea, pneumonia, and other diseases caused by exposure. A number of soldiers died en route to Wisconsin.

Madison citizens were curious about the newcomers. It was said that many waited for each new train's arrival to see the prisoners they had been told to expect, and they generally gave polite welcomes when the soldiers did appear. In a 1953 *Wisconsin Magazine of History* article, William A. Titus wrote that some Madison residents brought foodstuffs for the needy captives and made arrangements to supply second shirts to go with the rags on the prisoners' backs.

Still, no prison camp was pleasant for any soldier, let alone soldiers already seriously ill and suffering. In the weeks that followed the Confederates' arrival, death was a near-daily event. The local newspapers kept track; 31 prisoners died during the first week of May, and eventually the death toll would approach 140. Major Joseph A. Potter, an assistant quartermaster at Chicago's Camp Douglas, came to inspect the Madison camp and said he found conditions for prisoners "even worse than has been reported to me." In a 2008 *Wisconsin Magazine of History* account, historian Tommy Thompson found that judgment rather ironic, given that Camp Douglas had recently been found to be "a killing ground of pestilence."

Soon, Madison's squalid prisoner quarters were largely emptied and the Southerners transferred out. In their brief stay in Madison, Thompson wrote, the prisoners "probably experienced very similar treatment to that of prisoners in other camps, both good and bad.

"Perhaps the best we can say is that Camp Randall was no Eden, but neither was it the hell described at Camp Douglas in Chicago and many of the other prison camps."

But what of the nearly 140 who did not survive Camp Randall? They were buried at Forest Hill on the city's near-west side, where they would eventually be surrounded by some of the most prominent names in state history. And due to the efforts of a woman who devoted her life to their cause, the Southerners who might have unwillingly ended up in the North, in forgotten obscurity, are not only remembered but also respected to this day.

The woman was Alice Waterman. She was born in the South—in Louisiana—but lived in New York and other places in the North before moving to Madison in 1868. By then a widow whose business efforts had met with failure, Waterman worked as a housekeeper and, later, a landlady at the Vilas House Hotel in Madison, historian Thompson wrote. Eventually she discovered the then-unkempt resting place of the Southern prisoners. She thought they deserved better, so she took it upon herself to clear weeds and brush, mound the graves with dirt, plant trees, and put up a fence. She replaced dilapidated grave markers with new ones identifying the soldiers, their companies, and their dates of death.

For thirty years Waterman made the care of Confederate Rest her duty, doing whatever she could to improve the resting place of what she called "my boys." Eventually her dedication spread; Governor Lucius Fairchild encouraged her work, Thompson wrote, and city officials followed suit. When Governor C. C. Washburn, Fairchild's successor, joined a contingent of Union soldiers in placing flowers at the graves, he became the first Northern governor to lead a salute for former enemy soldiers. For years afterward, Memorial Day services were held at Confederate Rest, which the Confederate Veterans' Association called a "beautiful and touching tribute."

Waterman's love for her boys did not end with her death. When she passed away in 1897 she was buried at Confederate Rest. In June 1906 the United Daughters of the Confederacy placed a marble marker with her name and their thanks:

"Erected in loving memory by the United Daughters of the Confederacy of Mrs. Alice Whiting Waterman and her boys."

The marker was deep in snow the cold winter day I most recently visited Confederate Rest, after first walking among the ranks of Union dead. I brushed the snow off the Confederate Rest sign and off of the marker for Waterman, noting as I did the only sound drifting on the frigid January breeze. It came from mourning doves at a feeder in a yard across the fence, birds of peace now reigning among so many Civil War dead.

17

Where No Priest May Enter

Sauk City

Pine trees in country cemeteries are like coffee counters in bookstores or cats at B and Bs. It's almost a rule that they have to be there.

Even so, the pines at the Andrew Roll Free Congregation Cemetery in the countryside a few miles from Sauk City and Prairie du Sac are notable for their towering beauty and for their history, as well as for the way they alert a motorist that a cemetery is at hand.

It's an unusual one, at that, though there is little in the look of the burial yard to set it apart from so many other country cemeteries. There is a small chapel near the road, a sign with the cemetery's name, and tidy rows of traditional grave markers, yet the graveyard is in one significant way a most untraditional place.

The cemetery was established in 1863 to serve the burial needs of members of the Free Congregation of Sauk County, or "Freethinkers." Three years later, congregation member J. Ulrich Schmidt, assisted by ten-year-old Adolph Ochsner, went to the nearby Baraboo Bluffs to obtain pine saplings for the new burial ground. A century and a half later, the rows of transplanted saplings have grown into stately pine alleys that so distinguish the cemetery today.

One other thing that distinguishes the cemetery is its early bylaws that declared it to be clergy-free. Or, as the congregation's administrator Michael Whaley put it, the bylaws declared "that no priest or minister would ever be able to do his thing there."

The rule has been relaxed by time—"We have had ministers out there," Whaley says—but the prohibition was as much a part of the congregation's origins as those sapling pines. And it was completely in character for an organization founded "to unite the foes of clericalism, official dishonesty and hypocrisy, and to unite the friends of truth, uprightness and honesty. . . ."

The Sauk County congregation was modeled after the German *Freie Gemeinde* (Free Congregation, or Free Society), a movement brought to America in the mid-1800s. It did not begin as an antireligious movement, but it was zealously anticlerical. After the first U.S. *Freie Gemeinde* was established in St. Louis in 1850, the movement grew quickly; by 1852 there were twenty-six such groups in Wisconsin alone.

Photo by Dennis McCann

An "unknown" grave marker at Andrew Roll Free Congregation Cemetery in Sauk City, Wis.

Eduard Schroeter, who would become a pivotal figure in the Sauk County congregation, explained the Free Thought philosophy in a German-language paper published in Milwaukee. He emphasized the anticlerical bias by saying, "all authority rests in the congregation, and in it all its members, men and women alike, shall have equal rights. The foundation for the congregation shall be Reason, and the great teachings of nature and history."

The congregation would not exclude certain rites and ceremonies, however, "so long as they are not compulsory and are sensible and beautiful," he wrote. "We have no dogmas or decrees, fixed for all time, but only fundamental principles and general views of the world which are subject to continual clarification . . . we decree neither a belief nor a disbelief in God and immortality. We know of no priestly office as the sole bearer of the spirit and the truth, nor of a laity as mere empty vessels to be filled by it, as the Catholic and Protestant churches do, to a greater or lesser extent."

The Sauk County congregation struck a chord among many in the area, and the group prospered. In 1853, the year the congregation was officially incorporated, it held its first Thomas Paine celebration, honoring the American revolutionary whose writings on liberty, democracy, and the separation of church and state were an inspiration to German Free Thought groups. The group also began celebrating Spring Festival and its annual Founders Day, and while the congregation has changed in philosophy (it is now affiliated with the Unitarian Universalist Association) those three events still occur annually.

In 1857 the group built a new hall in Sauk City and, later, a school. In 1876 the congregation purchased Free Congregation Park, which would become the home of Park Hall, the historic meetinghouse that still serves the group today. Another meeting hall was established in Merrimac and a third at Honey Creek, on the same ground as the cemetery.

Freethinkers, mostly educated and middle or upper class, were heavily involved in Sauk County life and politics. One 1880 description of Sauk City called them "a sect of Atheists" who were met with initial opposition from others in the community but whose members constitute "a very respectable portion of the community." But in a 1998 look back at congregation history, Jane Eiseley noted that one of the Freethinker farmers near the Andrew Roll Cemetery was said to have been "surprised and wounded when the Reformed minister refused to return his greeting, and drove by in his buggy without looking at him.

"But the Freethinkers could be harsh too," Eiseley added, "as when Andrew Roll donated the land for the cemetery provided that no priest should ever set foot on it."

All programs at Park Hall were conducted in German until 1937, according to official congregation history. As late as 1940 there were still 111 members, but after World War II, membership declined; by the 1950s, the congregation sought affiliation with the American Unitarian Association in order to remain in existence. The merger was sometimes rancorous, and membership continued to dwindle for several decades before numbers actually began to grow again, in part due to a closer relationship, since 2002, with Unitarian Universalism.

Today, Whaley says, the group—the only surviving Free Congregation of some two hundred that once existed—is still growing and includes some who lean toward Buddhist thought, others who tend toward Wiccan beliefs, the traditional group of skeptics and questioners, and more. Its Web site notes that it still holds "what is very likely the longest running celebration of Thomas Paine by an organization or institution in the U.S.A., if not the world."

The hall at Honey Creek is still used once a year as well, Whaley said, usually for the Spring Festival. And the cemetery is still in use, serving almost exclusively members of the congregation, including the descendants of founding families. As for the pines, "We've lost a few," Whaley says. "The ones that are there, most of them seem to be in pretty good shape [but] I would guess in the next twenty-five to thirty years we will start to lose a few."

Perhaps they will, but for now those onetime saplings, like the remarkable and strong-willed congregation they served, stand as hardy survivors.

The Cemetery within a Cemetery
Hurley

It is the cemetery within a cemetery. While Hurley Cemetery spreads wide and deep on the southern edge of this northern border city, another burying ground next to the busy highway into town occupies a much smaller parcel, part of the whole but separated from it by a fence of stone and wood and by a weathered iron gate.

The smaller plot is Sharey Zedek, the Jewish section of Hurley's community cemetery and therefore something of a timepiece. Today you would have to search hard to find even a handful of Jews in Hurley, neighboring Ironwood, Michigan, or other communities along the onetime Iron Range.

But in an earlier era Hurley was home to more than the immigrant Italians, Finns, Poles, and others who came to find ore in the ground or fortunes in the forest. It was also home to a vibrant Jewish merchant class, immigrants whose names are remembered on headstones here in both English and Hebrew—Rosen and Sher, Cohen and Fink, Goldman, Tobin, and more.

Steve Heifetz, a Minneapolis cardiologist, didn't know all that when he and his wife, Andrea, decided to take a side trip to Hurley following a short vacation in Door County some years ago. Nor was he aware of Hurley's racy reputation a century earlier, as an unapologetic comfort station to the range's many miners and lumbermen. "Hayward, Hurley, and Hell" might not have been the official city slogan, but no one challenged its accuracy in the days when downtown Hurley was lined cheek to jowl with saloons, gambling emporiums, and, as Heifetz later put it, "an even older profession frowned upon in the Torah."

He would learn Hurley's story later, but it was his own story he was there to pursue. What he found would be just the first chapter in the larger story of a community.

I did not know about Heifetz or his search for roots when I first visited Sharey Zedek, but I later found an account of his genealogical journey on a Web site he created for the cemetery. The quest began, he wrote, after a blessing bestowed on his twins at their synagogue directed them to "Look back through us from generation to generation. From generations you have known, to generations we no longer remember."

Who were those generations? Heifetz asked himself.

He went to Hurley armed with the scantest of clues. His mother had told him that his grandfather, who had died when Heifetz was an infant, had graduated from Hurley High School. Thanks to a colleague who had noted a possibly related name on a Hurley stone, he knew that his grandfather and great-grandparents might have lived there years earlier. Heifetz and his wife arrived too late in the evening to begin the search for his roots at the Iron County Museum, so they went instead to Sharey Zedek.

In the fading light of evening they walked the rows past about seventy headstones. Eventually they reached a very old and worn tombstone shaped like an obelisk, on which they could barely make out the English name beside the Hebrew name: "Mrs. F. G. Rein, Mother, Died Sept. 12, 1917, Age 52 Years."

"I was standing," Heifetz wrote later, "at the grave of my great-grandmother. The first tangible proof my family was here. Likely the first family to visit her in over fifty years."

He took the stone they had carried with them from home and placed it atop the marker, fulfilling what he called the ancient

Jewish tradition to remember the dead. Only an hour in Hurley, and already Heifetz had made one exciting find.

There would be more. The next morning he and his wife pored over dusty old records in the Iron County clerk's office, discovering the 1897 deed of a house Moses and Fanny Rein had purchased for $350 on Copper Street. They found Fanny Rein's death certificate, which in turn yielded the names of her parents: Israel Feinberg and Mere Malko (Mariam) Feinberg. They rushed back to the cemetery and found Mariam's grave under another obelisk.

"I was standing," Heifetz said again, "at the foot of my great-great-grandmother's grave."

At that point they headed to the Iron County Historical Museum to learn more about the community where his family had lived. The county's original courtroom struck them as straight out of an old episode of *Perry Mason*, and the sometimes-sordid tales of old Hurley were, well, instructive, but the biggest surprise came after they toured mining, textile, and musical exhibits. There they viewed a religious display that included old sepia photographs of a woman and man. Again, it was Fanny and Moses Rein—Rabbi Moses Rein.

"Astounding," Heifetz thought. A rabbi!

And so the larger story unfolded, that of immigrant Jews, mostly from Lithuania, coming to the rough and woolly northern forests to run businesses that met the needs of miners and lumbermen and what families they had. The congregation of Sharey Zedek met first in homes of members, until eventually a synagogue with its distinctive dome was built. Moses Rein arrived to serve as rabbi in 1893, only months after immigrating to America, and served until 1921, when he moved to Minneapolis.

Through newspaper accounts and other records, Heifetz was able to piece together more of his family's story. He went to the house on Copper Street and talked with its current owners and later walked to Division Street to see the original synagogue. The synagogue, no longer needed after the Jewish population dwindled and the congregation faded away, had been converted to an apartment building in 1940, but Heifetz was able to walk its original wood floors and visit the former women's gallery. He met with local residents who remembered the days of Jewish services, which he knew must have seemed mysterious to some in the largely Catholic community. And he went back to the museum to hold the synagogue's original brass menorah, imagining Rabbi Rein lighting its candles for worship.

And still the chain of events that began that dusky evening in the cemetery played on. Heifetz learned from a Hurley attorney and history buff, Paul Sturgul, that after Sharey Zedek closed in 1940 many of its religious articles were passed on to a temple in Ironwood, but their later whereabouts remained unclear. After a story about Heifetz's discoveries appeared in the local newspaper, an antiques dealer remembered a trunk of odd—to him—items he had stored away, including cloths with six-pointed stars and foreign lettering that he had taken for Finnish prayer rugs. Thus did Heifetz and Sturgul recover the Torah scroll, prayer shawls, wedding canopy, and other items from Sharey Zedek. In 2005 Heifetz gave them to the Iron County Historical Museum for permanent display—but not until after his youngest son, Adam, had used the Torah cover at his bar mitzvah in Minneapolis. Heifetz estimates that Adam is the fifth generation to have used it.

The ceremony dedicating the museum's new display drew a nice crowd of local and state officials, a rabbi from Chicago, people with ties to Hurley's Jewish past, and the local historical society, and it all ended with a free meal, served with the assistance of the St. Mary's Catholic Women's Council.

Heifetz continued to research his family's past, even obtaining photos of the cemetery in Lithuania where other relatives were buried. On occasion he continued to pursue the trail of other artifacts from Sharey Zedek, and that search yielded more fruit. In 2008, the Torah from Sharey Zedek, then more than one hundred years old, was recovered from a storage shed near Ironwood.

"That," Heifetz said, "was the pièce de résistance."

The Torah, like the other artifacts, will live on as another relic of that earlier time. But Heifetz says a Torah is supposed to be used, not merely looked upon, so it was employed in a service in Minneapolis in 2008 and likely will be used for children's services in the future.

All of which is as it should be. History, after all, is a living thing, even when it is uncovered after decades among the dead.

19

Tales the Tombstones Tell
Richland Center

When I called to ask about her late grandfather, F. W. Fogo, and his encyclopedia-sized examination of Richland County cemeteries in the 1950s, Judy Vanstralen had just one question.

Was there something in there about a man killed by a whale? Vanstralen asked, scratching the rust off one of her distant childhood memories.

Certainly, I said. Nice coincidence, because it was Fogo's account of the one-of-a-kind marker that had led me to see it in the first place.

"Killed by a whale" was the inscription on a tombstone in Sextonville Cemetery for the unlucky James McCorkle, who was indeed killed by a whale in the Sea of Japan on May 25, 1848, at age twenty-five. McCorkle, as it happened, was buried at sea, but his family put a marker in what was then rural Wisconsin. Fogo found the marker more than a century later, and I visited half a century after that. The inscription had been almost erased by the years and the elements, but McCorkle, who had sailed six times around the world before that fateful whaling expedition, was still remembered.

I would never have known about him, though—or about the couple whose marker credited them with twenty-five children, or the woman so proud of her weight (450 pounds) that it, too, was etched in stone forever—but for Fogo's exhaustive research of Richland County cemeteries. The son of a newspaperman who was then editor of the *Republican Observer* in Richland Center, Fogo, accompanied by like-minded companions, spent years visiting the more than ninety cemeteries in his home county, reading stones, taking names, recording epitaphs, researching family stories, and eventually publishing columns on what he found.

"Tales the Tombstones Tell" ran from June 1955 through December 1959, with breaks when winter snows made cemetery inspections difficult, but it was not until late in his project that Fogo revealed his inspiration. That had occurred when Fogo—

Photo by Mark Fay

F. W. Fogo chronicled unusual gravestones, like this one in Richland Center, Wis.

his name was Stephen but he used F. W. for his byline—was in Mill Creek Cemetery and came upon the grave of his old friend, John Cook. Fogo wrote:

> If it had not been for him, we doubt if any of "The Tales the Tombstones Tell" would have ever been thought of and certainly you would not be reading one now but for a chance remark made long ago by Mr. Cook to the writer of these tales.
>
> It all started back before 1932. Mr. Cook, who spent part of his winters in Florida, had just returned from the south. There had been a large number of deaths during the winter among the older folks and Mr. Cook remarked that many of his old time friends had passed down the long, long road. He spoke up and said, "It has become so during the past few years that if I want to visit my old time friends, I have to go to the cemetery to do so."
>
> This writer thought of that remark and, as he had visited a few cemeteries and always found someone he once knew he made up his mind to visit, if possible, every burying ground in the county. There are 91 of these cemeteries and visits have been made, with two or three exceptions, to all of them.

This writer, to adopt the old style, didn't have five years to devote to one county. Nevertheless, one late autumn day, shortly after discovering Fogo's columns online, he—okay, I—set out to trace some of the columnist's footsteps through Richland County burying grounds.

I began at Bear Valley Cemetery in the town of Buena Vista, in the yard of what is now called the Brown Church, built in 1874. The cemetery dates to 1863, when the first lots were offered for five dollars each, though by 1881 the price had doubled. As Fogo had, I found graves of Civil War veterans and early pioneer farmers, and I pieced together some of their stories from clues etched in stone.

Robert Keppert, born in Germany, married Elizabeth Cheney,

born in England, and eventually settled in Richland County where, after Robert's Civil War service, they farmed. Elizabeth died in February 1903 and was buried under a marker promising,

> *In the soft light and sweet repose,*
> *Of that fair land of bliss,*
> *She calmly rests and waits for those,*
> *She loved and left in this.*

She did not have to wait long. Robert died one month later.

Fogo told the backstories of many of those who reside in Bear Valley, all interesting, but he missed one. I had learned from a previous visit that under a red-brown granite stone lies William C. Wright, father of the architect Frank Lloyd Wright. If he knew the connection, Fogo didn't mention it.

A few miles up the road was St. Killian's Cemetery, located behind a handsome old Cream City brick church from 1887. A fat, aged beagle howled from the house next door but seemed little threat, so I wandered up and down the rows, finding the graves of the Aspel infants Fogo had noted ("Two little flowers just lately given to bloom on earth, to bloom in heaven") and one that came later for one Francis Michael Mullen (1929–1999) that asked, "Why me?" Fogo would have liked that.

A larger curiosity was just as he had written. In an unusual formation, burials in St. Killian's run both east-west and north-south. Further, it was Germans who were buried from east to west and Irish from north to south. And sure enough, at the end of orderly rows of Germans the graves of Irishmen—Mullen, McNulty, Keaney, Dorgan, and more—were turned ninety degrees. Fogo asked his readers why, but if he found the answer he never shared it.

In Sextonville Cemetery, I found not only the grave of the unfortunate McCorkle but also that of Charlotte T., wife of W. J. Atwood, who died in 1864 at age forty-six and whose sad epitaph read, "Slighted on earth, But accepted in heaven."

Fogo didn't write much about another small cemetery I found

quite by accident near Dog Hollow Road and County NN. Stoddard Cemetery, a family plot set on top of a hill, hasn't been used since 1898 but was still nicely tended, wrapped by a small fence and with flags flying. Later, not far from Hoosier Creek, I stopped at Pleasant Hill Cemetery, which seemed not much of a hill but was the resting place of numerous Indians who had moved to Wisconsin to farm. One stone remembered the life of William Recob, a Civil War veteran who died in 1881 and whose stone suggested less-than-rigid faith in an afterlife.

"Gone," it read, "to find the unknown reality of another world."

As Fogo also had, I found Coumbe Cemetery off of Highway 60, up a gravel road behind a quarry. There was the grave of John Coumbe, whom Fogo called the first white settler in Richland County, and graves for a number of veterans of past wars. I was most struck by three matching headstones for the Crandall brothers, William, John, and Wilson, who all died in the Civil War. Fogo, it seemed, had been more touched by the sad marker for Olive Pilling, wife of Isaac, who died September 15, 1859:

She went not alone for on her breast,
A babe of an hour sleeps at rest.

Fogo's stories of the lives of old soldiers and settlers were informative, but he was clearly also struck by those who never had time to leave a mark. He would note poignant markers for children such as, "Our Hattie, 2 years, 1 month and 3 days. May we meet her in heaven," or young Alfred G. Taylor, whose life on earth did not stretch two years. His marker reflects the faith of his parents:

Sleep on Alfred and take thy rest,
God took thee home when He thought best.

In the end I had an enjoyable day among the dead, noting as Fogo had great old-fashioned names such as Ebenezer Young and Azubah Gewald and Gottleif Neugart, not to mention the revealing epitaphs. You can't do much better than, "Why me?"

Only at Sand Prairie Cemetery, on Highway 60, did I leave disappointed. I walked up one row and down the other, walked every row twice, but I never found the marker for Clara Washington, wife of John Burns, whose birth-death dates Fogo had reported as 1861–1908 and whose headstone reported her weight as 450 pounds. When he pursued that odd bit of information, Fogo found that Clara had developed a glandular problem that caused her to gain such weight that she required the services of eight pallbearers.

"Despite her weight," he wrote, "she was quite active and was evidently quite proud of her weight, else it would not have been recorded upon the tombstone for her in the Sand Prairie Cemetery."

Later, when I called his granddaughter, Judy Vanstralen recalled her grandfather as a small-town newspaperman who enjoyed people and local history—and knew where to find both.

"When I was a little girl we used to go on Sunday drives with my grandparents and sometimes we would visit cemeteries," she said. "What my grandfather liked to do was visit cemeteries."

F. W. Fogo died in 1962 and was buried in the Richland Center Cemetery, Vanstralen said, near a spot where a number of infants had been buried.

"I was told that he picked that spot because he wanted to be near the babies," she said. "I think that must have been near to his heart."

In reading his "Tales," I would agree.

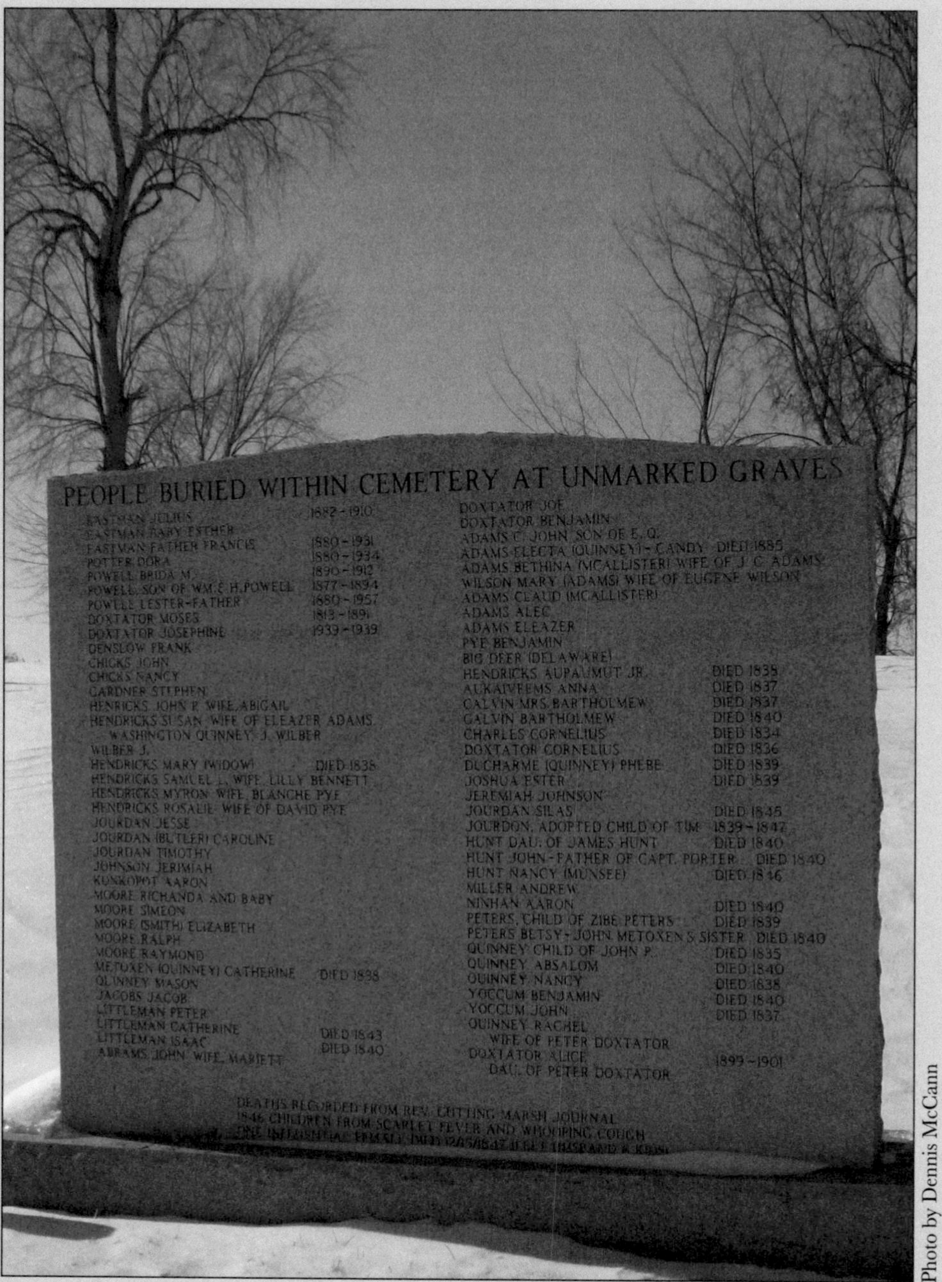

Photo by Dennis McCann

This marker in the Stockbridge Indian Cemetery commemorates those buried there in unmarked graves.

The Restoration of a Cemetery
Stockbridge

St. Mary Catholic Cemetery sits prominently on a slight rise on Moore Road on the north edge of town, just off the main highway that parallels the east side of Lake Winnebago. The cemetery has served the needs of Stockbridge Catholics since the earliest days of the community in the mid-1800s.

But there is another cemetery directly across the road, this one smaller and older than its Catholic cousin and a bit more removed from Moore Road—so removed, in fact, it is accessible only by a driveway across a farmer's property. It's worth the side trip, however, because the Stockbridge Indian Cemetery has a significant story to tell, one so notable that it is on the National Register of Historic Places.

Stockbridge, which bills itself as the Sturgeon Capital of the World, takes its name from the Stockbridge Indians who were part of a large-scale Indian removal from New York in the early 1800s. By 1825, Stockbridge and Munsee Indians—hence today's hyphenated Stockbridge-Munsee tribe—were occupying land along the Fox River at what is today Kaukauna. The migration continued for several years, and among the New York–born Indians who were moved to the frontier of what would become Wisconsin were Electa and John Quinney, siblings who were to become some of the best-known members of their tribe. They are among those buried in the Indian cemetery.

Electa Quinney, as some fourth graders might have learned in their study of state history, is known as the first public school teacher in Wisconsin. In 1828, because of her special interest in educating the children of her tribe, Quinney opened what is described as the first school in the state without an enrollment fee. For her contributions to reading and writing there is yet today a school named for her in Kaukauna.

The tribe did not stay long in Kaukauna, though. Shortly after the last of their party arrived in the region the federal government moved to establish them instead along the east shore of Lake Winnebago, in an area already populated by a small number of Brotherton Indians who had also come from New York. The struggle to find a permanent home for the Stockbridge was long and frustrating, and it was to this cause that John Wannuaucon Quinney devoted much of his life.

John Quinney was born in New Stockbridge, New York, in 1797. He made his first trip to Wisconsin in 1822 as one of a party of tribal members seeking land for resettlement, land they initially bought from the Menominees near Green Bay. An educated man and an orator, Quinney became a leading diplomat for his tribe over a period of decades, often negotiating land issues with the federal government and with other tribes.

Once in Wisconsin, Quinney drew up a new tribal constitution that called to replace hereditary chiefs with elected leaders, a change approved by members but not without some conflict from traditionalists. On one of his trips to Washington, Quinney addressed Congress in support of Indian self-government. He is credited with the first use of the term "Native American" in a political context.

"I am a true Native American, descended from one of those characters whose memory every American reveres," he said. "My grandfather David Nau nau neek Kannuck was a warrior and he assisted your fathers in their struggle for liberty."

In the 1840s the U.S. Congress made tribal members citizens and individual landowners, causing a split when Quinney represented some members who wanted to retain tribal status. In 1848 he helped negotiate a treaty that called for his people to move further west, but in 1852, when he was in ill health and thought himself too old and poor to move again, Quinney asked Congress to give him title to his home in Stockbridge. When he died in 1855 he was buried in the Indian cemetery there.

He never knew, of course, that the stonecutter misspelled his name on his grave marker, leaving the "e" out of Quinney.

If John Quinney succeeded in remaining permanently in Stockbridge, a large part of the tribe did not. While some members became citizens and won title to their homes in order to stay in the area, the remainder of the tribe moved to a reservation in Shawano County near Bowler, where they still live today.

In the tribe's absence, the cemetery became a historic footnote, and an overlooked one at that. Over time an adjacent farm encroached upon the cemetery property, which fell into serious disrepair. But in the early 1990s the tribe began efforts to regain control of the property and, when the effort was eventually successful, took extensive steps to rehabilitate the site.

"That was quite a project, maybe a couple years' project," said Doug Miller, one of the tribal members involved in the restoration. First the tribe had to reassert its legal control over the property. Then, they brought in ground-penetrating radar to identify the unmarked burials and establish boundaries that encompassed all of the graves. A large stone was placed at the entrance to the cemetery to identify known burials, marked and unmarked; a few new grave markers were set in the ground to replace broken or stolen markers (Miller said some local residents spoke of seeing grave markers from the cemetery at yard sales), and the cemetery was finally ready to be rededicated.

"That was quite a ceremony," Miller said. "They had a color guard there, and people from the tribe spoke. That was the burial place of the tribe when we came to Wisconsin. Well, it wasn't even

Wisconsin then . . . so that was kind of the point where the tribe from the east and the tribe here came together.

"At the time that it was done or shortly after, there were people from quite a ways away that came to see it. Most of them were like history buffs or people like that, and some of them were tribal members," said Miller, who added that working on the restoration helped him learn more about his own tribe.

Among those given new grave markers was Electa Quinney. Happily for the woman who had cared so much about education, the stonecutter correctly spelled her family name.

Photo by Dennis McCann

Electa Quinney is known as Wisconsin's first public school teacher.

Even in the Grave, He's Free

Rewey

The dead can't tell their stories, so their stones are left to speak for them.

In little Carmel Cemetery, which slopes away from the handsome white Carmel Church that stands amid tall oaks, the names on the markers are Williams and Jones and Evans—names that inform the visitor that this was part of the once-vibrant Pecatonica Welsh settlement. Unlike other groups who came to America, the Welsh brought only a few surnames, Williams and Jones foremost among them.

One marker, an obelisk that stands at the grave of one James D. Williams who died at the age of sixty on August 2, 1903, tells a story all its own:

"Born a slave in Virginia, Made Free by President Lincoln's Proclamation."

Now these are stones with a pretty good story.

The Welsh began arriving in this part of Iowa County in the 1930s, when lead was the magnet pulling settlers to southwestern Wisconsin. The first Welsh settler was thought to be William Owens, but families named Davies and Jones, Williams and Hughes soon joined him. The settlement was spread over an area that measured about seven miles by ten miles, its residents primarily occupied in mining and farming but united above all by faith.

At first, settlers held singing and prayer services in various cabins. Eventually, residents formed the Welsh Calvinistic Methodist Church, establishing a permanent place for worship. One of their own number, John Davies, would go on to preach the gospel for forty years, until his death at age sixty-three. Even as the Welsh immigrants adopted English as their official language, they kept their native tongue alive in worship, singing hymns in Welsh and praying their familiar prayers. Many of the oldest graves in the settlement's cemeteries carry Welsh inscriptions.

But James D. Williams, born a slave, of course did not come from Wales. The man known in the blunt style of the time as Negro Jim had come north to Wisconsin with members of the Pecatonica Welsh community who had fought in the Civil War. He made his home with Edward Williams and adopted his friend's name.

A history of the community, *In the Shadow of the Mines*, noted that James Williams no doubt suffered some resentment and discrimination because of the color of his skin, but also said the majority of the community apparently welcomed him. Williams, who like his new neighbors loved to sing, learned the traditional Welsh hymns and gladly raised his voice with the choir. He had a music box he played for children, raised vegetables in a large garden, and jokingly referred to himself as the only Welsh Negro in history.

But more than that, he was perhaps the only Wisconsin black man to own his own lead mine. Williams's mine was about three miles south of Rewey, and he would travel to it with his mule to dig for lead. Not until forty-five years after his death, according to *In the Shadow of the Mines*, was the mine discovered to contain measurable, if hardly profitable, traces of gold.

When James Williams died, an overflow crowd attended his funeral at Carmel Church.

Today both Carmel and its sister congregation, Carmel-Peniel Presbyterian Church, are still used for services, though Carmel, which has only woodstoves for heat, holds services solely in summer months. Services are no longer in Welsh, but occasional Welsh hymn singing, or *gymanfa ganu*, keeps the old traditions alive. And when that happens, it is tempting to wonder if the spirit of old Jim Williams, still a free man, hums along.

Photo by Mark Fay

Emmanuel Dannan's stepparents killed him when he refused to lie about their crime.

The Boy Who Would Not Lie
Montello

While passing through Montello one sunny summer day I pointed to a giant cottonwood that shaded the lawn, the sidewalk, and the street and told my wife—in this way I have of needing to share useless knowledge—that it was the largest tree in all of Wisconsin.

"How do they know?" she replied.

Lacking a good answer, I made one up.

"They just do," I said, but given the events of history there, you probably can take it to the bank.

In Montello, telling the truth matters. Some Wisconsin communities set aside special days to honor cranberries or cheese or even rutabagas, to march cuts of meat down Main Street to make tourists hungry, to hurl cow pies for fun and prizes, or—in at least two counties—to celebrate UFOs, even if most sightings have been outside of taverns at closing time.

But Montello once set aside a day to honor the truth. The event grew out of a tragedy from the state's earliest days, but its memory is preserved in Greenwood Presbyterian Cemetery a few miles out of town on County B, where a granite grave marker honors the legend of Emmanuel Dannan, 1843–1851, "The Boy Who Would Not Tell a Lie."

Dannan was a babe in arms when his parents moved to Milwaukee in 1843, as his story goes, and within a few years he was also an orphan. He spent time with aged relatives, in a parsonage, and later in a poorhouse, and he finally was given to the Samuel Norton family, which moved him to Marquette County.

Dannan's poor luck was not improved by his new circumstances. Norton was no bargain in the stepfather department. About 1850, Emmanuel was said to have witnessed his stepparents killing a peddler for his horse and wagon, and when the Nortons learned what he had seen, they demanded that he keep their heinous deed secret. Dannan, though, refused to lie for them, even when he was tied to the rafters of their cabin and whipped with willow switches thicker than a man's thumb.

"Pa," he said, "I will not lie."

But the truth could not protect him. Emmanuel Dannan died at age eight. He was first buried in a family cemetery plot and later moved to the cemetery across the country road from Greenwood Presbyterian Church, in a grave not far from the fence that separates the eternally sleeping from a cornfield. The Nortons were convicted for the deaths of both Emmanuel and the peddler and were sent to state prisons, and Dannan became a national hero for upholding truth. According to an account in the *Marquette County Tribune* a few years back, church groups in Milwaukee set out to erect a forty-foot-wide marble monument for him, but when contributions totaled just $1,099.94, a promoter was sent east to raise more money. He returned requesting reimbursement for expenses totaling—no lie, of course—$1,099.94 and disappeared, as did Dannan's story in short order.

In 1953 the story was revived by the *Milwaukee Sentinel*'s Charlie House, whose column made Dannan a hero all over again. In response, the Montello Granite Co. and Bittman Monument Co. of Milwaukee erected a proper marker honoring "The Boy Who Would Not Tell A Lie," and in 1954 Montello declared the first National Truth Day.

Truth is elusive, though, and the celebration was not held

again until 1980. In 2001, the 150th anniversary of Dannan's death, Truth Day was revived once again. The next year it was still alive; a Montello library assistant, noting the day's proximity to the election season made it "the perfect time" to honor truth, said third graders were being asked to write essays on the importance of being honest.

Even if, as the sad experience of young Emmanuel showed, it isn't always easy.

Photo by Mark Fay

Only the headstones were moved to make way for a parking lot at St. Mary of the Snows Catholic Church.

A Short Visit with the Belgians

Namur

The casual visitor could be forgiven for taking one look at the cemetery at St. Mary of the Snows Catholic Church and concluding that Belgians must all be very short people.

This is, after all, one of the most unusual, even head-turning, burying yards in all of Wisconsin. There are nearly seventy headstones crowded into the space one boastful Milwaukee beer baron would have taken for himself alone.

This bunch of Belgians wasn't always so bunched. Once upon a time they were buried in the conventional manner in a conventional cemetery space in front of the church, which sits on a curve on Highway 57 in southern Door County's farm country.

Then, about 1970, the church decided it needed a parking lot and selected the very space where the dearly departed had been parked for years. The stones were removed and replanted in a concrete slab adjacent to the church, about six inches apart. The bodies stayed where they were.

I felt bad when I parked on that asphalt surface one summer day, but what was I to do?

But for its mere bathtub-sized dimensions, St. Mary of the Snows is in every other respect very much a Belgian cemetery. This is not surprising, given that it is located in the middle of the most significant Belgian settlement in Wisconsin, perhaps in America. Walloon-speaking Belgians began to arrive in Door, Kewaunee, and Brown counties in the 1850s, establishing communities with such home-country names as Namur, Rosiere, Brussels, and Luxemburg. The region is still heavily Belgian (try Belgian trippe, a pork sausage made with tripe and cabbage, the next time you pass through Brussels).

Names on headstones in St. Mary of the Snows are similarly old country: Alexander DeGrand, Floratine Patois, Nicolas Joseph Jamquet, Antoinette Laduron, and Justin Chaudoir, the last "born in Belgium in 1842, died at Green Bay, 1902." In another touch common in Belgian cemeteries, some of the stones display photographs of the departed enameled or otherwise affixed to the marker. Chaudoir's glass photo shows a strong-looking man in apparent good health, with a thick mustache and dark eyes.

I was there too early in the day to go next door to Chris and Jack's Belgian Bar, where the sign outside urged, "Try our Belgian beers and chocolates." (From previous trips through the area, I can vouch for both as first-rate, though Belgian trippe is more an acquired taste.) Duty and another cemetery called anyway, so I headed north—and then immediately turned off onto Cemetery Road.

Country roads come by their names honestly. Expect to find boards for sale on Lumberyard Road, and County Line Road is always a divider, not a uniter. So I knew what I would find on Cemetery Road. The only surprise was that it lay just past the intersection with Dead End Road, which seemed a bit redundant.

This cemetery, also largely populated by Belgians, was outside of St. Francis Xavier Catholic Church, but this time the dead and their markers had been left undisturbed. Again, a number included glass photos of the deceased, most wearing formal dress and expressions that suggested the people being photographed knew where the images would go.

Names included Wautier and Neuville, Jeanquart and Renier and, as always, hinted at lives lived long and lives cut woefully short. At one point I realized that all of the markers around me were

Photo by Barbara McCann

What you see is what you get on many country roads.

for infants; one had a teddy bear etched in the granite surface but only one date to mark both birth and death. Others bore etchings of lambs; another stone, brightened with plastic flowers, read, "Little Angels are hard to find," while yet another for a girl who lived but eighteen months read, "The 'tiny rosebud' God picked to bloom in heaven."

Sadly, some of them could have fit in the abbreviated plot I'd just visited.

I learned later that the more than fifty infant graves were clustered together because of church policy that prohibits unbaptized persons to be buried in consecrated ground. John M. Kahlert's *Pioneer Cemeteries* said such sections are usually small and set apart but that the infant section at St. Francis Xavier was larger than most and more conspicuous.

It was that. I didn't know any of them, young or old, but through the rest of that bright summer day those children's stones on Cemetery Road stayed in my mind, grave upon grave, row upon row.

Photo by Mark Fay

Shantyboy Hill got its name from loggers, like Hans, who lived in rough shanties in the woods.

24

Shantyboy Hill
Presque Isle

There are two paths leading to the little cemetery known as Shantyboy Hill. One is short and direct, around the ball diamond and down a little hill to the graveyard. The other is longer and much more interesting. It follows a nature trail on a wide loop through the woods and, near the end, past a stand of waist-high ferns. Most visitors take the shorter route, but to me the more difficult trail just seemed the right way to approach Shantyboy Hill.

Lord knows the loggers who rest there had a tough go themselves.

The community known today as Presque Isle wore a few other names in its nascent days when the first settlers came to the big woods of northern Wisconsin to carve out a living. Around 1900 John J. Foster operated a sawmill there, and the settlement was called Fosterville, but only until William S. Winegar became resident lumber baron, when the community's name was changed to Winegar. Those were the rough-and-tumble days of the northern pinery, back when oxen might have done the heavy lifting but men and boys were still left with hard and dangerous duty in the forests.

Shantyboy Hill is both resting place and memorial to those loggers, who got their nicknames because they lived in rough shanties in the woods. The cemetery is home to a few dozen small white crosses, some bearing names—"At Rest–Hans, 1867–1914"—

and some with no name for the onetime lumberman buried below. One Arthur Wm. Peterson, who lived to the ripe age of twenty-five, is remembered by name, as is Joseph Grogg, a true survivor who was born on Christmas Eve in 1854 and lived until April 1923.

The dates on Clark Nokes's cross, 1906–1917, show that he had no such luck. The math is sobering. Nokes was a child in an era in which children were too soon asked to be men. According to a history of the area by local resident Gladys Hill, one day he skipped school and went to what was called the lumber mill's "hot pond." The pond tender on duty had just fallen into the water. He asked Nokes to watch the logs while he went home for dry clothing, but when he returned Clark Nokes was nowhere in sight. Thinking Nokes had just walked away, he didn't report the boy missing.

His parents searched for him when he didn't come home that night, and the next day Clark's body was found in the hot pond. Because there was no cemetery in Winchester, where the family lived, Clark Nokes was buried in what was then still called Winegar, laid to rest in the company of loggers. Eventually the town built a new cemetery, and the small clearing where Nokes and his companions had been buried became neglected and overgrown.

Years later, though, the cemetery was given new life, if that isn't a contradiction. The brush was cut, grass was mowed, and a rail fence and welcoming sign went up. The Chamber of Commerce offered a prize to the fourth-grade student (fourth graders study Wisconsin history) who came up with the best name for the plot. "Shantyboy Hill" was the winner.

The sign at the entrance notes, "As lumbermen they lived in shanties in the woods. They were the workers who cut our forests, rode the logs, broke the jams and often died in doing those things."

In the 1940s, as the onetime lumber town of Winegar was in transition to becoming the more tourist-friendly Presque Isle, the old hot pond was converted to a fish-rearing pond. The days when "timber!" rang through the woods were gone forever, even on Shantyboy Hill.

Photo by Mark Fay

Young Clark Nokes drowned in a lumber mill's "hot pond."

Peshtigo Fire Cemetery
Peshtigo

Cemeteries in northern Wisconsin were seldom the highest priority of early settlers. Food and shelter were typically first concerns, but eventually need for burial places would arise. Death and taxes, after all.

In 1908 in Conover, in Vilas County, just for one example, Hildegard Turnquist became the first member of Pioneer Lake Lutheran Church to die, and so today the community still uses Hildegard Cemetery, named for its inaugural resident.

In Peshtigo, in what is now Marinette County, the need for a burial site was multiplied a thousand times and more in just one horrific night, October 8, 1871, when the most deadly and damaging forest fire in North American history roared through northeastern Wisconsin and Upper Michigan. It was as if the flames were sparked in hell and blown on devil's breath, so awful was its destructive force, and in its ashen wake the number of dead was more than twelve hundred—maybe many more—and property damage was in the millions.

And so the Peshtigo Fire Cemetery came to be, a burial site that still today draws thousands of visitors who walk its solemn grounds and visit the adjacent Fire Museum to learn more about the conflagration that dwarfed the Great Chicago Fire—which, coincidentally, burned that very same day—in lives lost and damage done. As chapters of Wisconsin history go, the Peshtigo Fire was as significant as it was terrible; when the State Historical Society of Wisconsin approved the very first historical marker in 1951, it was erected there.

Some wonder today how a fire could grow so large and uncontrollable, but remember that the rough lumber towns of northern Wisconsin at that time had little firefighting equipment or training, even as fire posed a constant danger. Intense drought had left the north even more vulnerable than usual that year, and the land-clearing practices of the time had left ample timber slash as kindling on the forest floor, awaiting only a spark.

The wind would supply that. Small fires had broken out for days in advance of the big one; the thick smoke in Green Bay was said to have left the days dark as night even before cyclonic winds lit the woods on fire on October 8. The wall of flames spread so quickly that some isolated farms and camps were engulfed before residents could do anything to save themselves. And as the fire was further fueled, it spread exponentially.

Refuge was scarce—and often turned out not to be refuge at all. Some who sought safety in wells or small ponds were boiled to death. Buildings burned before residents could flee, and the pace of the fire overtook many who sought to outrace it. Many of those who did survive submerged themselves in the Peshtigo River, clinging to floating furniture or even horses and cows, raising their heads above the surface only long enough to gulp another breath of hot air. One of those who survived in that manner was a Catholic priest, Father Peter Pernin, who later wrote *The Great Peshtigo Fire: An Eyewitness Account*, which still is widely read for its recounting of the drama and destruction.

The Peshtigo Fire Museum, open each year from May through the fire anniversary on October 8, is on the site of Pernin's church, which was lost in the flames. The building was the first church to be rebuilt after the fire, as a Congregational Church at a new site. It was moved to its present site after a rebuilt Catholic Church also was lost to another fire in 1927. The church has been home to the museum since 1963. It houses extensive accounts of the blaze and its aftermath, plus a few artifacts that survived the fire—among the most important is Pernin's tabernacle, which he brought to the river in an effort to save it, only to find afterward that the strong winds had knocked over the wagon and blown the tabernacle onto logs in the water.

But the cemetery tells its own sad story to anyone who passes the sculpture of roaring flame, walks through the fence gate built some years ago to deter vandals, and roams among its markers. The most notable is a large monument erected in 1981 to mark a mass grave for as many as 350 victims who were so consumed by the fire that none could tell man from woman from child. As many as seventy-five were thought to have died in a boarding house on the east side of the river; others were found dead with no trace of burn marks, but without identification, either.

Individual grave markers and interpretive signs tell more personal stories. The last burial in the cemetery was that of Sebastian Zimmerman in 1916. He was buried next to his wife, who had died in 1894. Both are listed as survivors of the fire, but one can only imagine the memories they took to the grave.

A broken stone remembers Henry Merkatoris, who was one of a handful of men who heard the church bell sound a fire alarm and went to the edge of town to try and stop the flames. Mrs. Merkatoris waited until the fire came into the city, but when Henry did not appear she feared he was lost. She gathered their five children, fled into the river, and clung to logs. In the morning, she saw him returning through the smoke and ash. He died ten years later in 1881, at age fifty-one.

That was about as close as Peshtigo got to happy endings. Terrance Kelly, his wife, and four children lived in the Upper Sugar Bush and were separated when the smoke and wind arrived. Terrance had a child in his arms; his wife had another. The other two children clung to each other. The next day Terrance and one child were found dead nearly a mile from his farm, but all the others lived. Terrance and Terresa, age two years and two months, were buried together. "Both died Oct. 8, 1871."

Even on a bright summer afternoon more than a century later, the stories can darken a mood. This is not a cemetery filled with those who lived life long and to completion. A sign tells of the two Mellen children, whose nineteen-year-old brother walked them into the icy river and ducked their heads repeatedly to escape the fierce heat, only to bring them ashore dead of hypothermia. And another tells of Charles Lemke, who loaded his family onto a wagon to flee the fire. Perhaps he did so too quickly, because his wagon was not properly hitched. When he stopped his horses to fix it, a wave of fire washed over the wagon and his family in it. John S. Pratt lived until 1882, but his marker nonetheless describes him as "Victim of the Peshtigo Fire," not survivor, because even the living forever carried scars from the fire's wrath.

Another stone spared the details but couldn't soften the outcome. "All Lost," it reads, "in the Calamity."

Catharine, Murdered by William
North Andover

It was my fault that a day that had started so slowly should turn so hell-bent-for-leather. At first the sun was high, and time my friend; a few breaths later it was late afternoon and, not for lack of searching, I still hadn't found Catharine Jordan.

It was the goats' fault. I'd left home plenty early to reach the little corner of southwestern Wisconsin where I had heard Catharine Jordan was buried. I made such good time along the way that I decided to waste some. When I got to Fennimore and found a livestock auction under way, I stopped to see what was selling.

Goats were. Thirty-six little dairy goats in the first lot.

"If anybody wanted a project to take home," the auctioneer had said, "this is it."

Real livestock men would have snickered, but I found the goats cute as all get-out, just bleating and blatting as they bumped around the ring. Not so cute as to inspire my hand to go up, though. I've done dumb things at auction—who hasn't?—but even I knew that if I drove off with thirty-six dairy goats bleating in the backseat I'd get home with the biggest case of buyer's remorse since the last guy bought a Gremlin.

So I sat on my hands (it's a scientific fact that your head itches more when it's not safe to scratch it) through the sale of sheep and goats, a wonderfully whiskered old ram, a few calves, and finally a pig that looked so much like Babe the movie pig that I decided it was time to go.

Then I headed up the road to Boscobel before I finally checked map over memory and saw I was heading in the wrong direction, so I turned south again along the Wisconsin River, enjoying the bright sun and keeping an eye out for turkeys. Where the Kickapoo meets the Wisconsin I saw an eagle, a big one in a tree on the opposite bank. Eventually the eagle lifted off and flew lazily away. You'll seldom see a turkey do that. When I came across a small flock a few miles later they just wobbled heavily toward cover, and I looked out at a horizon broken only by silos and steeples.

And cemeteries! Right. So I pushed on and soon reached North Andover, where a letter writer had told me I would find the grave of Catharine Jordan and "add a touch . . . of intrigue to your day."

Photo by Mark Fay

Catharine Jordan's grave is said to be the only one in Wisconsin that gives murder as the cause of death—and names the murderer, William Kidd.

So far the intrigue was that I couldn't find it. And I really wanted to, because the story—yes, this is what you've waited for through the longest buildup since the Old Testament—is a good one. Her grave marker is said to be the only one in Wisconsin that gives murder as the cause of death—and names the murderer to boot.

But as small a town as North Andover is, I couldn't find the grave. I drove up First Street and down Second, traveled along Canal Street and Main Street, and then ran clean out of streets. North Andover had never grown to need more. So I started driving country roads that led off like spokes, looking for the only landmarks I knew of—a white marble stone in a small cemetery with a fence and gate.

On Oak Road I found a cemetery with a fence and gate, but no Catharine. In the midst of my futility I at least found diversion: eagles were everywhere, having come over from the Mississippi River to scour for roadkill or dead baby pigs discarded by farmers. We all like to think eagles are noble hunters, one man said when I stopped his tractor to ask for help, but they like their food dead and ready to eat just like the rest of us.

Time was wasting, so I asked at the lumberyard as well, to no avail. I stopped at strangers' houses and again struck out. One person told me that a man who wrote a book on North Andover (I'm guessing it's just one volume) might know, but he didn't live there anymore. And I was about ready to give up and head home when I did what I should have done at the start. I went to the tavern.

Bingo. Bartender Mary Mergen knew just what I was talking about, so I followed her directions and a few minutes and miles later found Ramsey Cemetery, where even before I got out of the car I could see the name *Jordan* on a marker in the back.

All these decades later, it still was chilling to read the deed etched in stone: "In memory of Catharine Jordan, murdered by William Kidd, June 15, 1868, age 21 years, 3 months, 6 days."

The story had been passed on through the years and occasionally made the papers, which explained the clipping my reader friend had found and kept for maybe forty years before passing it along. As it goes, Kidd—not Billy but William—and Jordan were from pioneer families in North Andover and eventually courted. Kidd was supposedly hot for marriage, while Jordan was not. On the night of June 15, 1868, she went for a buggy ride with Kidd. The next morning she was found beside a road a mile from her home, her throat slashed.

Kidd disappeared, which didn't stop a Lancaster justice of the peace and six jurors from declaring him guilty of murder. Later, Kidd was taken into custody in another state, but while being returned to Wisconsin he drank a vial of poison he had secretly brought along and died shortly after.

Kidd was said to have been buried in Lancaster. It was too late to go see his grave, but I thought maybe someday when I pass through again I'll stop and look for his marker, too. It would be a grisly bookend for Catharine's own sad one.

The Man Who Isn't There
Spring Green

The grave of the man often called the world's greatest architect is itself something of a work of art.

An irregular-cut limestone marker stands at the head of a stone slab that serves as grave cover, while a glass and metal marker informs the who and when—Frank Lloyd Wright, 1867–1959. Tall pines rise all around, and but for voracious mosquitoes this little burying ground near Wright's former home and studio at Taliesin would seem a restful place.

Wright was brought to the cemetery at Unity Chapel after his death at age ninety-one, his coffin carried to its final resting place. Surrounding his grave are those of some of his family, including his mother, Anna Lloyd-Jones Wright; his former mistress, Mamah Borthwick Cheney; two of her children; and other relatives. Because Unity Chapel is within sight of the heavily visited Taliesin complex, many who go there in search of the Wright experience probably seek out his grave in Jones Valley and stand at the foot of that slab, taking photographs, maybe even paying respects.

If so, they'd best speak loudly. Wright isn't in his grave, which proved to be his home not for eternity but for a mere twenty-six years. In March 1985, at the behest of his widow, Olgivanna, Wright's body was secretly exhumed, cremated, and shipped to Taliesin

West in Arizona. By the time the story broke in the *Capital Times* of Madison there was nothing to do but decry the brazen act. Many of his Wisconsin admirers and followers did exactly that.

Karl E. Meyer, a former Wisconsinite, wrote in the *New York Times* a few weeks later that the "body snatching" was "equivalent to uprooting Jefferson from Monticello for reburial in Beverly Hills." A former Wright apprentice, David T. Henken, called it "almost a sacrilegious act . . . an obscene thing to do to any person." Even the Wisconsin legislature weighed in, passing a resolution calling Wright's exhumation "a historic, cultural and economic loss for the community and state, depriving residents of Wisconsin and future Wisconsin generations of this heritage."

The legislature's "tut-tut" resolution, as one writer later called it, was "barely heard outside the state Capitol." And like all other pleas for Wright's return, it was roundly ignored in Arizona.

Interestingly enough, it was in Arizona that Wright had died in April 1959. Despite his advanced age, few close to him suspected he was anything but healthy. In *Frank Lloyd Wright: A Biography*, Meryle Secrest wrote that at a picnic of the Wright fellowship at Taliesin West, Wright looked a bit pale but seemed otherwise fine. That night Wright complained of stomach pains and was treated for an intestinal obstruction at a Phoenix hospital. Two days later his condition was rated satisfactory, but early in the morning of April 9 his night nurse reported, "He just sighed—and died."

Wright's followers and relatives made plans to immediately return his body to Wisconsin, Secrest wrote. Wesley Peters, Wright's son-in-law and trustee of the architect's foundation, drove a pickup truck to Spring Green with Wright's coffin in the back, covering eighteen hundred miles in twenty-eight hours. The coffin was placed on a cloth of red velvet in front of the great stone fireplace at Taliesin.

Then, just as sunset approached on Sunday, April 12, the old bell at Unity Chapel began to toll. The coffin was carried to a waiting wagon, draped in more red velvet, and covered with flowers. Two black Percheron horses pulled the wagon the half mile to Unity

Chapel and the waiting grave. Olgivanna, Wright's third wife, was among the relatives and friends who trailed the coffin on foot. The Reverend Max D. Gaebler of Madison's Unitarian Church, where Wright was a member, read several prayers, including readings from the Book of Job, concluding with, "Thou shalt come to thy grave in a full age, like as a shock of corn cometh in his season."

Secrest wrote that it was stated at the grave that this would be a temporary site, because Wright had been working for more than a year on plans for a new chapel that would adjoin Unity Chapel "to serve as his memorial and final resting place." Design work was almost complete, and in the weeks before his death Wright had put the finishing touches on what he called "Unity Temple." The temple would serve both as a place of contemplation, Secrest wrote, and as a repository for Wright's remains as well as those of Olgivanna, their daughter, Iovanna, and members of the Taliesin Fellowship. The first steps to building it had already begun; the footing was marked off, and blocks of stone were hauled in from nearby Rock Springs Chapel.

Work on the temple never went beyond that, however, perhaps because Mrs. Wright preferred Taliesin West and the Fellowship's emphasis had shifted there. She was said to have seldom used a bench placed near the grave for her convenience.

Olgivanna died March 1, 1985, in Scottsdale, and it was her dying wish that Wright's body should be retrieved, cremated, and interred with her own ashes. Because they expected opposition, members of the Fellowship moved "secretly and with dispatch," according to Secrest. No one might have noticed if John Patrick Hunter of the *Capital Times* had not been tipped to the move. The story broke too late to prevent the body from being moved, but in plenty of time to spark uproar.

"The sneaky way it was done was particularly bad," said Jack Howe, a former Wright apprentice who was by then an architect in Minnesota. "They left the cemetery a mess, did not resod or level the ground, just threw some soil in the grave and replaced the stone marker. I was very angry when I saw it . . . I think moving the body was inexcusable, even if Olgivanna did request it."

Wright's son David called the act "grave robbing," saying Olgivanna selfishly wanted Wright's ashes, and other Wright followers argued there was no other place than Wisconsin, particularly the Wisconsin River Valley Wright had so loved, for the architect to spend eternity.

"We've lost the spirit of the valley," said Robert Graves, son of a caretaker at Wright's farm. And Wright's oldest granddaughter, Elizabeth Wright Ingraham, also an architect, told an interviewer, "The heartland is where Frank Lloyd Wright's spirit is. That's where the largest body of his work has been done. I think he wanted to be buried there."

Still, more than a few interested parties imagined Wright himself enjoying the drama he was able to create even from the grave. The actress Anne Baxter, another granddaughter, called the grave opening "painfully absurd."

"But then," she added, "he may be laughing for all we know, because his spirit is much bigger than his bones."

And, almost a decade later, George H. Bechtel wrote in the *Wisconsin State Journal* that—wherever his spirit reposes today—Wright might appreciate the construction of the long-debated Monona Terrace Convention Center in Madison as well as the popular "heritage tour" of such Wright designs as the S. C. Johnson building in Racine, the Seth Peterson cottage at Lake Delton, and Madison's Unitarian Church, especially given that the tour is called "Wright Here in Wisconsin."

"That he isn't," Bechtel wrote, "but his spiritual fancy may be tickled by all this activity. We don't know for sure, of course, because you can't learn from an urn in Arizona."

The Disrupted Spirits of Wisconsin Point
Superior

Not long before I arrived in Superior I had watched a wonderful public television program on cemeteries, including the rather famous boneyards in Key West and Atlanta that I've visited and written about in the past. The upshot was that cemeteries are not just sad homes for the dead but often places of intriguing history and architecture where visitors can honor the memories of the departed.

But not always.

In Wisconsin's most distant northern corner is a peninsula that reaches into Lake Superior. It is called Wisconsin Point (across the way is Minnesota Point) and is a popular spot with hikers and especially birders. Long ago, it was home to a band of Ojibwe, or Chippewa, people. Even today, near the tip of Wisconsin Point, a sign identifies the site of the old Chippewa burial ground, not far from a plaque on a stone that was once part of the Interstate Bridge.

The sign doesn't tell the real story, and the marker only hints at it.

"Here was," the marker reads—and note the verb tense—"the burial ground of the Fond du Lac Band of the Chippewa People dating from the 17th century. It was removed to St. Francis Cemetery, Superior."

Even that acknowledgment doesn't do justice to the injustice.

Wisconsin Point is at the entryway to Superior harbor. Early in the twentieth century the city wanted a huge dock there to load iron ore into Great Lakes carriers, along with railroad access and homes for workers. To build it, they had to first remove the remaining resident Ojibwe from their longtime home on the Point, along with the cemetery said to hold the remains of three hundred people.

Government officials argued that the Indians had ceded the land in the Treaty of 1854, never mind that some had stayed there for another fifty years or so. One resident was the cemetery's caretaker, Joe Levearsh (his name is spelled differently in various accounts), who had lived with his wife in a hut on Wisconsin Point for nearly forty years. His nephew, Charles Drew, vowed to "die fighting" the move, and the Superior newspaper reported the tribe had held a "war council" to discuss resistance because "seven generations and more lie buried in this cemetery," including at least one chief, O-sa-gie.

Not satisfied with taking the land of the living, said one removal opponent at the time, now the white man wanted the land of the dead.

But in the end the residents—most of the dead and all of the living—were removed. The bodies were put in a mass grave near the Nemadji River in Superior, but no care was taken to see they would not be further disturbed. Later, the slope on which they had been reburied was undercut by construction of a road, according to Superior historian Ron Mershart. Bodies and decayed clothing spilled toward the river.

"It's just one of those sad things," Mershart said, in conscious understatement.

Back at Wisconsin Point, the sandy ground turned out to be no place to construct an ore dock, so none was ever built. Instead, the peninsula became city park space, except for the tip where a lighthouse and Army Corps buildings were constructed. Today, as visitors drive onto the point to take in the terrific views of Superior and Duluth across the water, to hike, or to watch for migrating birds, they are greeted by a historical marker that recalls Longfellow's "Gitche Gumee" and asserts, "starting in 1666, and for nearly 200 years, explorers, fur traders, miners and missionaries journeyed along this south shore in bark canoes."

Notice any group missing there?

Near the end of the point is the sign announcing the Chippewa burial site and the stone marker, covered with items left by visitors through the years: beads and feathers, stuffed animals, walking sticks, coins, tobacco, and more. One bag was labeled "asema," the Ojibwe word for tobacco, and offered, "Help yourself."

Ironically, there are still Indian remains at Wisconsin Point. By some accounts, only about 180 of the most identifiable graves were removed, and the current marker is only an approximation of the original site. Some say the road now passes over some buried remains, and, according to Dennis Peterson, a Fond du Lac tribal attorney, those who do know where their ancestors were buried often won't say.

"I'm told these secrets are passed on from generation to generation," he said. Visits are quiet affairs. Gary Johnson, a Lac Courte Oreilles Chippewa who directs the First Nations Center at UW–Superior, added that not many visitors or area residents know the full story of Wisconsin Point.

"Most people," he said, "weren't even aware of the history of that thing [or] why the tribe wants to get it back. A lot of people don't want to know about these things."

That may change. A few years ago the federal government declared the site surplus property and offered it to other agencies. The Bureau of Indian Affairs stepped forward, asking to take possession on behalf of the Fond du Lac Band. The tribe's petition, citing long historical ties to Wisconsin Point, was eventually approved. The tribe intends to find uses for the eighteen-acre site that will memorialize those who were there before.

Perhaps then Wisconsin Point, where the pines crowd close and create a solemn and silent backdrop, will be the place of quiet repose that the disrupted spirits deserve.

When Peaceful Rest Was Washed Away

Bayfield

When a sewer construction crew discovered human bones—a female's partial thigh, a partial upper arm bone, a partial male pelvis bone—beneath a downtown street in 2007, they were surprised, of course.

But there was no great mystery, certainly not a case for "Bayfield: CSI."

City officials immediately surmised the bones had been deposited by the cataclysmic 1942 flood that had so badly damaged the downtown of this little Lake Superior community—and which had washed out part of Greenwood Cemetery, disinterring bodies, breaking open caskets, and disrupting what was supposed to have been the eternal peace of the grave.

"I can remember seeing those caskets laying there and some bodies hanging out there," Jim Erickson recalled in 2009. He had rushed to the cemetery that 1942 morning after hearing the news. "I took off and went running back to the farm. I was only twelve years old. It sticks in my mind very clear. I can still visualize it."

Cemeteries are meant to be permanent places. But the floodwaters that ravaged Bayfield on July 18, 1942, disturbed the sleep of both the living and the dead. More than eight and a half inches of rain was reported over a twelve-hour period, creating a raging torrent that rushed through the city's big ravine into its business district.

The flood washed out roads and tore down telephone and telegraph lines. It flooded buildings with sand and debris and water, destroying a handful and damaging dozens more—the drugstore, the food store, the bakery, the post office, the Blue Ox Tavern. The rushing waters carried along boulders as big as horses, upended railcars, and left boats high and dry. And, odd as it seems with all that water, fires broke out, demanding the full attention of the city's firefighters and fire chief Ed Erickson, who was Jim's father.

But when word came that a section of Greenwood Cemetery had been let loose, even fire took a backseat.

Bayfield Heritage Association

A cataclysmic 1942 flood washed out part of Greenwood Cemetery in Bayfield, Wis.

"I left everything [downtown] and went up to the cemetery," Ed Erickson said years later. "And holy, it was a mess up there."

The cemetery sat high on a hill overlooking the city. The land had been a gift to Bayfield from early resident Colonel Isaac Wing, who in 1888 donated ten acres for a city cemetery and five more across the road to the Catholic Church for their own burial ground.

The extensive flood damage and recovery efforts made news across the state. The local *Bayfield County Press* labored to keep up with developments, but the newspaper's own building was a victim. When publisher William G. Reque explained why the first accounts were late and somewhat abbreviated, he noted that the paper's press and other equipment were "buried in five feet of sand topped by a goodly supply of rainwater, well stirred and caked to a beautiful chocolate brown.

"We know you will forgive our delays," he wrote, even as he thanked newspaper executives in Washburn and Superior for helping the *Press* in its hour of need. "Such is the spirit that makes this newspaper game something more than just a business—something that you can't quite give a name to—but it's something that makes you want to go on in spite of 'hell and high water.'"

Subsequent stories highlighted just how much hell the high water had visited upon Greenwood Cemetery. Recovering the disgorged bodies and returning them to resting places was left to a crew of area morticians, led by Harvey L. Gildersleeve of Bayfield and fire chief Ed Erickson.

"Everyone realizes that many folks have put in a strenuous time during the past few days," the paper noted in its July 23 edition, "but few can appreciate the efforts of the valiant crew of men who have taken the responsibility at the cemetery . . . certainly the most difficult job within the entire community."

> They have been on the job from the beginning, working all hours, and under the most trying conditions. In spite of the fact that they have received little local assistance . . . and were constantly annoyed by spectators they have been as patient and obliging as conditions would permit.

Then the reporting took on a scolding note.

> Periodically they had limited assistance but at no time have they received the local cooperation they deserved. This is one of Bayfield's greatest problems and we must recognize it as such. Let us be thankful that we have outside friends who, better than we, realize what we are up against. An Ashland delegation of businessmen came over Wednesday to lend their assistance on the cemetery job. We only hope that Bayfield won't forget that.

What the *Press* never reported in detail was just how grisly that work was. It wrote at length of other aspects of the city's recovery, from disaster funding and road repair to restoring communications and giving out hundreds of typhoid shots. And in a column headlined "Flood Flotsam—The Lighter Side," Jim James described efforts by would-be voyeurs to make their way past guards to see the cemetery damage.

> Among the few who succeeded, and considering the number who tried, relatively few gained their point, two women and their male escort, who represented themselves . . . last Saturday as being staff members of the Detroit Free Press, take first prize for gall and unmitigated nerve. Any cub reporter knows they'd have no such assignment at such a late date, but they got by with the idea until they encountered the morticians. Then the jig was up.

Among those guarding the road to the cemetery, the paper noted, were three local women, Eleanor Knight, Mildred La Pointe, and Margaret Winbigler, who "not only looked nifty, but carried on a vexing job with a veteran's efficiency [and] handled their billy clubs with dexterity. Someone has said that a policeman's billy club is close akin to the old rolling pin, not only as to shape but in its potentialities as well."

The best account of the sad duty at the cemetery came from Erickson decades later. In a most helpful local history project, a series of interviews videotaped shortly before his death allows the salty-talking former boat captain to speak from the grave.

The work was hard, he said. Gildersleeve had to attend to several funerals that same week, and another mortician suffered blisters from his boots. Eventually they had almost two dozen bodies "sitting in boxes and stuff. The stench was getting kind of bad so we started burying them.

"We were there, oh, seven days and six nights," he recalled, and permitted a small smile. "That's the only time the state ever bought liquor for anybody. They sent the health officer up. He said you have to have a little stimulant. I remember him bringing us a couple of jugs."

The main effort ended on a Saturday, but Erickson said he decided to go back up to the cemetery on Sunday and look further down a ravine. He had walked about a hundred feet, he said, when he came upon a woman's silk stocking. Upon further inspection the stocking was revealed to contain a woman's leg, separated at the hip.

"And as I recall," he said, "I don't think there was a run in that silk stocking."

Then he found a man's body, half submerged in the debris. "I dig around, I finally get his torso loose. A-number-one shape. With a green necktie on. All he had on was a green necktie."

In the end, most of the forty or so uprooted burials were identified and reburied. Those who could not be identified, either total or partial remains, were buried in a long mass grave. The final morticians' report to the city described the unidentified: "remains of a very short man, bald head, white fringe of hair on edges"; "remains of an adult male, about 5'6," blue suit and tie. Suit purchased from Seigel Bros., Superior, Wisconsin"; "in this grave were placed one male skeleton intact and is absolutely unidentifiable."

Miscellaneous bones were also boxed up and reburied, and while some bodies went unidentified, they were reburied with due respect, if also in everlasting mystery.

"That woman with the silk stocking on, we put her back in

there," Erickson said. "But to this day you can never find out who the guy was . . . with the silk necktie on. I've never been able to find out who he was.

"All he had on was that green necktie. He had to be an Irishman, I suppose."

A Veteran and Preacher Receives His Due

Eau Claire

All over Wisconsin there are unmarked and long-forgotten graves—even entire cemeteries—and most will remain that way for as long as time goes on.

But the grave of William Robinson, with no stone to tell even his name for more than eighty years after his death in 1923, met a happier fate. And good for that, because William Robinson, born and sold as a slave, later a Civil War soldier, and finally a respected Methodist minister in Eau Claire, deserves to be remembered. In 2004, when a few men dressed in the garb of Union soldiers joined local veterans officials, history buffs, and a few dozen others to place a stone marker at Robinson's grave in Forest Hill Cemetery, the man known as "the Great Colored Evangelist" was given his due.

"The march of this soldier is over," said one of those wearing Union blue. A bugler played a mournful "Taps," cannon fire sounded, and a wreath of evergreens was placed on his grave.

"William H. Robinson, 28 IND CAV," the gleaming marker reads.

Finally.

He was born William Cowens in Wilmington, North Carolina, taking the name of his first owner and master, Tom Cowens. Years later, as a free man, he changed his name to Robinson. According to "The Great Colored Evangelist," a history project published in 2008 by University of Wisconsin–Eau Claire student Abbie Withbroe, much of what is known about Robinson's life came from a narrative of his slavery days that he published in 1903. In *From Log Cabin to the Pulpit, or, Fifteen Years in Slavery*, Robinson told of watching at age ten as his father was taken away to a Richmond slave auction and of unsuccessfully fleeing his owner and later being sold—for $1,150—at Richmond, just as his father had been.

"His tale is one of a catalogue of horrors, blood, brutality and family break-up during slavery," another historian later wrote of Robinson's narrative, "as well as his service, first as a servant to his Confederate master who is killed in the war and then as a Union soldier."

Robinson's "service" to the Confederacy after war broke out was as a cook, according to Withbroe. After Union forces captured his unit in 1863, Robinson later wrote in his own account, he joined the Northern effort as a soldier, first for an all-black Massachusetts regiment and later for an Indiana unit.

"I was mustered out on December 29, 1865," he wrote, "with no home to go to, no starting point or object in life."

After the war, Robinson moved around and tried various occupations, but in 1877 he underwent a religious conversion that eventually led him to become a Methodist minister. He both preached and lectured extensively, often using accounts of his life in slavery as the basis for his talks, especially after his narrative was published. An invitation to preach in Eau Claire led him to move with his daughter, Marguerite (his wife and two other children had died by then), in 1910. By the next year the *Eau Claire Telegram* was calling him "the noted Negro evangelist."

Robinson wrote later that other ministers warmly welcomed him to Eau Claire, where he would live out the rest of his life. They were "men who at once became interested in my daughter and self," he noted, "and seemed to have no thought of the 'black rubbing off.'" He was affiliated with Lake Street Methodist Church, worked with the YMCA and the Salvation Army, and preached in other small communities in the region until he died in 1923, at age seventy-five. Marguerite paid ten dollars for a burial lot at Forest Hill Cemetery, but, for whatever reasons, the grave was left unmarked.

And it would be yet today, if not for a local newspaperman who wrote about Robinson in 2002. Jerry Poling cited the curiosity of a UW–Eau Claire history professor who had discovered Robinson's book and wondered how he had come to Eau Claire and, if he was as significant as the record showed, why there was no marker. Poling agreed, writing, "If we had walked in his shoes, we would know that he deserves—at the very least—a stone to mark his grave."

It wasn't easy, given government bureaucracy and official rules, but that stone was eventually produced. The Eau Claire County veterans services officer, Clif Sorenson, and others in his office became involved because, as Sorenson said later, "as a veteran, an unmarked grave is just intolerable to me." A major hang-up was that no records could be found to document Robinson's military service, which was not unusual for freed slaves who joined the army without being officially mustered in. Eventually, though, Robinson's autobiography was judged as sufficient evidence of his service, and a marker was procured through the Department of Veterans Affairs in Washington.

Then, in May 2004, men in the uniform of the Eighth Wisconsin Infantry joined veterans affairs officials at the grave for the long-deferred service. There was nothing on the stone to tell of the too-long wait, but at last Robinson was remembered for what he had done, and for what his story meant.

"Though he died eighty-one years ago and remained those years in an unmarked grave here at Forest Hill Cemetery," Sorenson told those assembled, "we, the living, can still do the right thing."

"William Robinson was given a memorial service deserving of a Civil War soldier, eighty-one years after his death," Withbroe wrote. "It was one of the only times Reverend Robinson's life was remembered by the people of Eau Claire, Wisconsin, since he walked the streets of the city."

Photo by Mark Fay

St. Joseph Catholic Mission on Madeline Island is the burial place of many Ojibwe Indians.

A Controversial Burial Ground
La Pointe, Madeline Island

Madeline Island is home to one of Wisconsin's most interesting and historic cemeteries—and perhaps one of its most visited, even if it is tucked between a marina for fancy pleasure boats and a line of summer cottages set on Lake Superior's edge. It is a burying ground that sits on the fine line between its intended duty as sacred place and its later role as tourist attraction.

It should not be a surprise that conflicts can result.

But then, when St. Joseph Catholic Mission established the cemetery in 1836, a dozen years before statehood, no one felt the need to consider what kind of neighbors the little graveyard would have in future centuries. The mission, which had been developed under the guidance of the famed pioneer priest and later bishop Frederick Baraga, needed a graveyard as part of its work among the island's fur traders and early residents, many of mixed-blood heritage, and for the large community of Ojibwe, or Chippewa, Indians for whom the island was a seasonal home.

Because so many Christianized Ojibwe are buried there, including one of the most important chiefs in the tribe's long history, the graveyard has long been known simply as the Old Indian Cemetery, even though some whites and mixed-blood residents are buried there as well. (And while the name was inaccurate, its use persisted for tourism marketing efforts for many years.) Among those buried in the cemetery is Michel Cadotte, who ran a fur-trading post for the North West Company and later the American Fur Company. Cadotte married the daughter of Chief White Crane. Her Christian name was Madeline, and so it became the island's name as well.

A worn marker identifies the burial place of the Ojibwe leader known as Bezhike, or Chief Buffalo, who was principal chief of the Lake Superior Ojibwe for nearly half a century before his death in 1855. He remains an iconic presence among the residents of today's Ojibwe communities at Bad River and Red Cliff, many of whom are his direct descendants. Chief Buffalo, who was born in 1759 and lived to the age of ninety-six, helped negotiate several treaties on behalf of his people, including one that required him to travel to Washington in 1852 when he was more than ninety years old.

Chief Buffalo converted to Catholicism—by some accounts on his deathbed—which allowed him burial in the mission cemetery.

Because of its historic significance, the cemetery has long had protectors. In 1953, Hamilton Ross, author of *La Pointe: Village Outpost on Madeline Island*, contacted the state office that handles historic sites designations, seeking an appropriate marker to place at the cemetery. "As you no doubt know," he wrote, "the burial ground in question is not, strictly speaking, a Chippewa cemetery, although it is commonly called 'the Indian cemetery.'" Many mixed-bloods were buried there, Ross said, "along with any Indians who might have been baptized in the Catholic faith." While another Catholic cemetery had long since been established, "the Indians and the mixed-bloods all seemed to prefer the old burying ground, and it is still used by them."

The mission cemetery was always a place of curiosity for island visitors, in part because of the custom of building small wooden structures over graves to shelter provisions—food, tobacco, a flint for starting fires—for the four-day journey to the spirit world. Before European contact, according to Steve Cotherman, site director at the Madeline Island Museum, the shelters would have been a simple bark structure, closer to a crude wigwam than the more traditional houses that tourists later found, which could suggest they were built long after the burials in an effort to "spruce up" the cemetery for visitors.

However, there was nothing to protect the structures themselves against the often-harsh Lake Superior elements. The cemetery's appearance suffered, to the point where visitors became disappointed, or even angered, at what they found there. In the early 1950s one critic described the cemetery as in "a state of pitiful dilapidation," but little came of it.

So the criticisms continued. In 1963 a postcard showing the cemetery neatly mowed and with intact grave houses was mailed to the Wisconsin Historical Society in Madison. "Dear Sirs," recent island visitors had written, "We would hope—as former Wisconsin residents—that the burying ground looked like this! It doesn't! We were there three years ago—and not a thing has been done to restore it."

A historical society official wrote back, assuring the couple "that I feel just as badly about its condition as you do." (Cotherman notes that until recently even many historians and archaeologists viewed native burial sites the same way they did Christian cemeteries, instead of considering their unique historical, cultural, and religious aspects.)

The next year another letter arrived at the historical society. "Dear Sir: After viewing the Indian cemetery on Madeline Island we departed with a feeling of disgust and a sense of shame for your society, in fact the entire state of Wisconsin, as never in all our travels throughout the U.S. have we seen such a disgraceful sight." They were unable to walk through the high grass, the letter's writers said, and there was much litter and rubble, headstones were tipped, and grave covers were rotting.

Adding to their disappointment was the fact that tourist literature at the time invited visitors to take in a story more than two hundred years old, promising, "As you browse through this peaceful spot you will be treading the sacred ground of the long distant past." One tourist publication in the early 1960s declared "On Madeline

Island, 'Spirit Houses' Contain Bones—and Ghosts—of Redmen," but in giving directions the text also noted the cemetery was "in a state of disrepair and neglect." Nevertheless, a society official replied that the state had no authority over the cemetery. Because St. Joseph did not have funds to maintain the cemetery, ownership had been transferred to Bad River in a trust agreement with the Army Corps of Engineers, which then built a breakwater to protect the cemetery against Lake Superior encroachment.

A letter writer in 1979 made the same complaint, and in 1986 a New York visitor noted, "Here was this historically significant cemetery that was broken down and overgrown. And within 200 yards was over several million dollars worth of yachts and the yacht club." And when another letter of complaint arrived in 1988, Jean Weber, director of the Historic Sites Division, replied, "Your reaction to the Indian cemetery is a common one."

> You have described appropriate customs for our culture: the flowers and neat plots of perhaps a New England . . . church yard. The Indians believe in a return to earth. What may look like neglect to you is a deliberate ritual of recognizing the slow and inevitable changes in nature—decay of material substances. Religious services and ceremonies to commemorate the spirit of both past and present life take place there regularly.

To be sure, some responsibility for the dire state of the cemetery lay with the intrusive tourists themselves. Today, if asked, museum staff will answer questions about the cemetery, attempting to present it in historical context as a complex cultural site, and urge visitors to the area (where Ojibwe Memorial Park, the marina, and the cemetery are found) to look from outside but not to enter the graveyard. In the long term, Cotherman said, the museum would like to work with the Catholic diocese and the tribe to agree on a plan to preserve and interpret the site.

That would be a sensible course for a sensitive place. The cemetery will always be of interest to island visitors, but it should be viewed more as artifact than attraction, a setting that speaks of island history that should not be forgotten. The Ojibwe were long ago displaced from Madeline Island to reservations elsewhere, but the spirits of those in St. Joseph's Cemetery should be respected now and tomorrow.

Spirits of the Dead Live On

Brussels

Given that the central belief of a Spiritualist church is that life continues after the "change" called death, it might seem a glaring contradiction to have a Spiritualist cemetery.

Then again, where better to communicate with the dead than where death is not thought of as an end? When I visited White Star Psychic Science Church in rural southern Door County, I half expected the nearby church cemetery to be filled with chatter, even on a snowy winter's day. That it was church-quiet instead may say more about what I brought to the meeting than about the psychic beliefs and abilities of church members.

This classic white country church, set on a quiet road a few miles off a main highway often clogged with tourists, has been active for well over a century, and Spiritualism has been practiced in the region even longer. A group of Belgian veterans brought the new religion to Door and Kewaunee counties after the Civil War. Interest in Spiritualism was high at the time; according to White Star Church's own published history, the heavy casualties of the war might have increased interest in communicating with deceased loved ones. This was a time, after all, when even Mrs. Abraham Lincoln consulted mediums, hoping to communicate with her young son Willie, who had died in 1862.

Spirits of the Dead Live On

In northeastern Wisconsin, Spiritualists attempted to raise the dead through séances. Desire LaCourt and his brother-in-law, Frank Jaque, who turned an old house into a church for their psychic services, led one sect: the French Spiritualist Church in Kewaunee County. That group continued into the 1920s when, according to the White Star history, one member cut off his hand to test the powers of his belief.

When he died, so did the church. All that remains today is the French Spiritualist Cemetery, an unmarked cluster of graves on the shoulder of a road outside Luxemburg, overseen only by the dairy cows in the field behind a fence.

White Star Church was built near Brussels in 1888 by John B. Evearts, a onetime Green Bay tavern owner whose wife had become critically ill. When medical doctors could not help, Evearts sought the services of a DePere spiritualist medium thought to possess healing gifts. When Evearts's wife recovered fully, the medium told him that he, too, had the gift of healing and prophecy and that if he would only give up the sale of demon rum he could become a great speaker and healer.

Before long, Evearts switched careers. He developed a modest following for Spiritualist services in private homes.

In such a heavily Catholic area, Evearts's conversion was frowned upon by some, including the pastor of St. John the Baptist Catholic Church in Brussels, who declared that no one could communicate with the dead—not even a priest—and forbade the practice. Again according to a history of White Star Church, a one thousand dollar bet was made between a Spiritualist believer and the priest over whether Evearts could indeed communicate with the spirit world.

More than one hundred spectators turned out at the home of an impartial local resident on the appointed day in June 1885, most of them Catholics eager to witness—and no doubt win—the showdown. Evearts was there on time, but the priest was a no-show until a horse and buggy was sent for him, at which time he denied any bet had been made.

"As a result of this debacle," the church account said, "the priest lost more than 40 families from his congregation who then followed Evearts, becoming Spiritualists."

To house the newly enlarged congregation, White Star Church was built on the site where it still stands today. By 1917 the church had some three hundred members. While today its membership is much smaller, the congregation still meets on the second, fourth, and fifth Sundays of each month, except in winter when the church is closed. (Outhouses provide little comfort in cold weather.) The church believes that all individuals have some level of psychic ability "and with practice, commitment and strong desire can learn to develop the Gifts of Spirit for themselves."

There are actually two cemeteries associated with White Star Church. One, appropriately enough on Cemetery Road, has a single large stone to mark a communal grave for a reported thirteen people, some of them children and infants. That burial ground proved to be on bedrock, so a new cemetery was established on County Highway K, where the earliest headstones date to the 1880s. Names on markers include Laviolette, Herlache, DeWarzeger, Delveaux, Debroux, and Corbisier. Also buried there is Leonard Delsart, who died at sea June 13, 1942, at age twenty-six, while serving as radioman for the United States Coast Guard on the U.S.S. *Escanaba*.

"Hero of the N. Atlantic," his stone declares.

He must have had quite a story to tell. But no matter how long I stood and listened, I couldn't hear him tell it.

Photo by Barbara McCann

Acknowledgments

I came up with the title of this book years before I got around to collecting the stories to fill it up—an enjoyable task but one that was certainly not a solo mission. Many who contributed to the making of *Badger Boneyards* are beyond the reach of a thank-you, and I wouldn't want to disturb their forever sleep anyway, but others deserve my gratitude, and so they shall have it.

Thanks to Kathy Borkowski of the Wisconsin Historical Society Press for buying me lunch and, even better, buying the idea of a book of cemetery tales, and to Michelle Wildgen for being both a gentle and a capable editor, always a good combination in that job. And hosannas to Don Newton, Apple genius extraordinaire, for patiently teaching an old dog new tricks, and then teaching him again.

My friend John Gurda proved a delightful guide one frigid winter's day at Forest Home Cemetery, a place he knows better than even the Grim Reaper. Thanks to Ginny Hall for the tip on the Cameron tombstones—and for good directions—and to Dick Baker for doing the legwork that fleshed out that tale. Much appreciation to Steve Cotherman and Sheree Peterson of the wonderful Madeline Island Museum for separating fact from fiction at that island's historic burial ground. In Medford, Pep Simek was gracious enough to share the creation story behind Tombstone Pizza. In Eau Claire, Clif Sorenson provided the records behind the effort to give Civil War veteran William Robinson the grave marker he deserved, a cause that began with the newspaper stories of Jerry Poling. And in Menomonie Carolyn Ohnstad was kind enough to introduce me to the long-departed lumber barons of Evergreen Cemetery.

Thanks as well to Jack Holzhueter for the brainstorming, mostly his, and to Ron McCrea for his help on the empty grave of Frank Lloyd Wright. Steven Heifetz generously shared the personal story of discovering his family's roots in Hurley. And in my hometown of Bayfield thanks to Bill Gover, Marilyn Van Sant, and Marilyn Winterer, who opened the archives of their beautiful museum to tell of the Bayfield flood, and to Jim Erickson for walking through the door at just the right moment and for agreeing to remember when.

First, last, and always, thanks and much love to my wife, Barb, for merely everything.

Index

Page numbers in *Italics* refer to illustrations.

Index

Index

Y

Z

About the Author

Photo by Barbara McCann

Dennis McCann is a Wisconsin native and longtime explorer of the state's nooks, crannies, and, yes, its burial grounds. A University of Wisconsin-Madison journalism graduate, he worked at several smaller newspapers before joining the *Milwaukee Journal* (later the *Milwaukee Journal Sentinel*) in 1983 as farm writer and state rover, a beat that eventually led to a career of traveling nearly every Wisconsin highway and most of its byways in pursuit of stories and travel columns. His previous books include *The Wisconsin Story: 150 Stories/150 Years, Dennis McCann Takes You for a Ride*, and *Rough Stuff*, a collection of his columns from *Wisconsin Golfer* magazine. Now a freelance writer, he spends most of his time with his wife, Barb, a retired teacher, at their home on Lake Superior in Bayfield.